STOP
APOLOGISING

STOP APOLOGISING

SILENCE YOUR INNER CRITIC, FIND YOUR CONFIDENCE, STOP SAYING SORRY

Tara Rule

authors
AND CO.

First published in Great Britain in 2024
by Authors & Co.
www.authorsandco.pub

Copyright © Tara Rule 2024

Tara Rule asserts the moral right to be identified as the author of this work in accordance with the Copyright, Designs and Patents Act 1988.

ISBN 978-1-915771-72-8 (paperback)
ISBN 978-1-915771-73-5 (hardback)

All rights reserved. No part of this book may be reproduced or transmitted in any form or by any means, electronic or mechanical, including photocopying, recording, or by any information storage and retrieval system without the written permission of the author, except where permitted by law or for the use of brief quotations in a book review.

For my girls
x

CONTENTS

A Note from Tara	i
Foreword	ii
Congratulations	iv

PART ONE	**1**
Your Apologising Rules	3
1. Why We Keep Apologising	6
2. You Are Not the Only One	19
3. Let Me Introduce You to Dobby	25
4. You Had One Job	44
5. Choose Your Inner Cheerleader	64

PART TWO	**87**
Stop Apologising Stories	95
Sorry for Not Replying Sooner	96
Sorry Dinner Is Late	98
Sorry for Crying	101
Sorry, but I've Just Got a Question	104
Sorry, This May Be a Stupid Question	107
Sorry for Interrupting!	110
You're Too Aggressive	113
Sorry Versus Thank You	117
Conscious Competence	119
Asking for Feedback	124

Confidence Stories	132
R — *Remember What You Are Good At*	138
U — *Use Your Strengths*	150
L — *Large Vision*	161
E — *Exciting Goals*	172
S — *Strengthen With Hope*	185
PART THREE	**201**
Let's Build Some More Hope Together	206
The End Is Just the Beginning	228
How to Find Me	239
Acknowledgements	241
References	243
About the Author	245

A NOTE FROM TARA

I have spent years helping clients and colleagues to stop apologising and feel more confident. Even better, I am now teaching my own kids, which is so amazing.

I was out for dinner last week with my husband and two girls who are ten and thirteen. One of my daughters turned to me and said, "Mum, you've taught me two things that I think are brilliant: one is to say thank you instead of sorry, and the other is that when you're cooking, if you can see any metal at the bottom of the pan, it means something's not cooking that could be!"

She said this completely unprompted. The grin on my face was huge! For years I've heard people apologise when they don't need to. I was full of so much love and pride that my daughter was aware and was choosing a different way.

I'm ridiculously excited for you to read this book. There are no more cooking tips! But I have crammed it full of ways to help you to stop apologising. Use it to silence your inner critic, find your confidence and stop saying sorry.

Enjoy!

Tara

FOREWORD

Sarah Brummitt, Executive Coach and Author

When we start out in our careers, we need to become experts in our field. Technical expertise gets us so far. However, that is *never enough* for us to succeed. Professionals are in the business of communication. No matter our role, our industry, our place of work, our experience, our seniority, or our expertise, we must communicate well.

This has never been harder.

We operate in a business environment forever changed by Covid-19 and we must step up our communication to build and strengthen our professional relationships and to get – and keep – our audience's attention. The delivery, length and quality of our message must be crisp, concise and compelling. Why? Because most people aren't listening most of the time. We live in a world of distractions and our attention spans are falling like stones so the words we use, how we sound and how we put it all together *really matter*.

Tara Rule is a life force, a natural coach, an engaging communicator, and someone to whom we all need to pay attention. Her focus on the use of the unnecessary apology is perfection because research suggests that the 'average Brit' says sorry eight times a day. Tara's book is essential reading. It challenges us to reflect on how, all too easily, we use the wrong verbal strategies to convey empathy, connection and humility… and how it works *against* us, rather than *for* us.

Seriously, enough with the 'sorry'! 'Sorry' isn't the way we should interrupt others, 'sorry' isn't the way we should preface sharing our point of view, 'sorry' isn't the way we should preface asking a question and 'sorry' isn't the way we should finish a contribution.

Read the book; enjoy the book; apply Tara's ideas from the book.

You'll *never* be sorry that you did.

CONGRATULATIONS

First, massive congratulations for taking the first step to stop apologising, silence your inner critic, find your confidence and stop saying sorry. This is a step towards a more confident you, a step towards a happier future.

I have spent a lot of my eighteen years in Tech, noticing my colleagues and clients apologising.

"Sorry for interrupting!"
"Sorry, this may be a stupid question."
"Sorry, I know everyone else knows what's going on but…"
"Sorry for taking up your time."
"Sorry…"
"Sorry…"
"Sorry…"

So often, I would let people know (in a kind and supportive way) they were doing this and they'd respond with, "Sorry! I know I say sorry all the time, but I just don't know how to stop. Sorry!" Does this sound at all like you?

I highlighted to a colleague, Hannah, that I heard her apologise all the time. She was completely aware that she did this *a lot* so we had a couple of conversations in a coaching style. Thanks to her willingness and determination to change, she was able to put a stop to this.

The impact of apologising too much can be huge.

- Colleagues are less likely to listen to you because you've just told them you're asking a stupid question.
- You are less likely to get that pay rise you're trying to ask for because you're too busy apologising for taking up your boss's time to ask confidently for what you want.
- And at home you're trying to do it all and feeling stressed because there would be too many apologies that you don't want to make if you, heaven forbid, put yourself first!

Back in 2018, I posted this on LinkedIn:

"Any recommendations for speakers for Adobe's Women's Network on the topic of *Stop Apologising*?"

I thought I'd be inundated as so many people apologise when they don't need to. I met some great speakers from that post, including an amazing woman who then became my coach. But not one person said they were an expert for *Stop Apologising*.

A few years later I still hadn't found anyone, despite the topic resonating with many and people often telling me that they apologise too much.

I realised that the speaker needed to be me! Actually, not only did I want to speak about it, but I also wanted to write a book about it. That way, I wouldn't just help the fifty people in the audience, but instead thousands, tens of thousands, millions of people on this topic that strikes a chord with so many of us.

The problem goes so much deeper than saying sorry in meetings. The bigger issue is what we say to ourselves. Are we saying sorry for being ourselves? Apologising for living? For taking up space? For not feeling good enough? What are *you* saying to yourself?

Have you (like so many people) ever said or thought that you're stupid or not good enough, that you have to be perfect or don't deserve to be where you are? That you're 'lucky'? I know I've said quite a few of these to myself *a lot* over the years.

I have mentored and coached thousands of people over the years. I know we all have that little voice inside our heads. You may call it your imposter, your limiting beliefs, or the negative voice in the back of your mind. I'm going to call it your inner critic, who says, "You're not good enough," or, "You don't deserve this." That voice telling you that you have to be perfect and you have to be liked. Your inner critic is saying these things to keep you safe. And once you are aware of that, you can choose to let it hold you back, or choose a different narrative instead.

I chose the subtitle of this book quite deliberately. But silencing the critic doesn't mean putting it in a box and trying to ignore it! You silence it by listening to it, thanking it and calming it down. When it feels listened to, it will feel happier. Then, and only then, will it quieten and give your inner cheerleader the space it deserves.

I have been through this process myself. I can guide you now, because I know what it's like to feel I'm not good enough. I have looked confident to others while having major self-doubt on the inside and I almost let fear get in my way of living a life I love.

You are aware that you apologise too much and you'd love to be more confident. Going through this book will help you reframe what you say to others, and even more powerfully, you will identify what you say to yourself and how to reframe that too. You will see that you can put your inner cheerleader in charge instead of your inner critic.

There is not a set book of rules in life. There is not one right way to sound more assertive, to be more confident, to be you. We all have our own experiences, stories and beliefs, but I am Tara Rule, so it is only right that I share with you some of the *Rules* I live by so you can create Your Rule Book™. I will ask you questions as we go so you can reflect on what you learn and think about how to apply it to your personal situation.

Over the years, I have created many Rules and I share them with my clients: Your Prioritisation Rules, Your Goal Setting Rules, Your Communication Rules and many more. In the course of this book, I will share with you three Rules:

- Your Mindset Rules.
- Your Confidence Rules.
- Your Apologising Rules.

You will be able to use them straight away to create Your Rule Book™.

I'm a qualified Professional Coach and I'm also a qualified Positive Psychology Coach. But I hadn't even heard of positive psychology a couple of years ago.

Positive Psychology
(term)
the scientific study of what makes life most worth living.

It is relatively new in the field of science and I simply summarise it as: Focussing on what's working rather than what's not working. It focusses on strengths, nurturing what you're good at and increasing wellbeing. Why? Because happier people are healthier, more productive, more optimistic and achieve more.

This book will not bamboozle you with science and psychology, but it is worth knowing that positive psychology is the foundation of much of my thinking. I hope to help you on that upward spiral of positivity of growth and development.

Before starting my own business, I grew my career to become a top-performing Commercial Director with a large global role in a big tech company. I had a team of thirty and the responsibility for everything from setting the strategy, deciding our priorities, managing headcount and costs, engaging our people and knowing where we were from a sales perspective every day of every quarter.

It was a fun, varied role and I loved working with so many different people. But then I found something I loved even more… coaching. I combined them for many years. I worked full-time and coached while also developing myself, starting my own business and being a mum.

I now coach people across the globe, online and in person. I love seeing people grow and take control of their lives. Every day I coach busy professionals and business owners to help them elevate their confidence, find their balance and live their most fulfilling lives. Plus, I help business leaders inspire and motivate their teams by running workshops and team meetings and by speaking at events. And I love, love, *love* what I do!

You will often see me with my head stuck in a book soaking up new information to help me and my clients. I love a good book recommendation so let me know your favourites! (You can find out how to get in contact with me at the end of this book.)

I have written this book because this message is so valuable and I want to share it with as many people as possible. I have helped my coaching clients get amazing results by putting an end to saying sorry and now it's your turn.

There are so many benefits to having more confidence: you'll progress your career quicker, you'll step out of your comfort zone more, you'll feel more motivated. You'll communicate better and speak up more. And you'll go after your dreams and take that leap of faith to believe in yourself.

I wasted years telling myself I was lucky and feeling I wasn't good enough, despite my successful career. I have invested thousands in myself, doing the deep inner work to realise why I believed these things and what I could do about my inner critic. I have overcome most of these false beliefs and have even had coverage in national newspapers about me. Amazing things can happen when you overcome your inner critic and grow your inner confidence.

Imagine talking with confidence. Imagine feeling confident. Imagine having such confidence that you don't feel the need to apologise. Imagine believing in yourself and backing yourself. Imagine confidently achieving all that you want in life.

What would you do with more confidence? What would you achieve? How would life be different?

If you are more confident at work, this will also positively impact those you work with. Think about it. Do you prefer it when your boss is in a good mood or a bad mood? When you show up happier and more confident, those you work with benefit. Focusing on your development makes you feel like you have more purpose, so you feel happier at home. This impacts your loved ones and sets a great example for kids if you have any.

An investment in yourself, whether of money or time (like taking the time to read this book), creates a ripple effect on those around you. The benefits are endless.

When you stop apologising and sound more assertive, people will take you more seriously and have a more positive picture of you. You will be able to negotiate better and make more of an impact, and you'll feel happier because you don't start every sentence with an apology that makes you feel bad. What other benefits will you discover when you stop apologising?

I interviewed my friend Hannah when I started writing this book and she told me, "I realised it was a habit, but I also felt like I didn't deserve to be where I was. But now 'sorry' is no longer my go-to word; I know the value I bring and I'm so much more confident being me! I'm even teaching and empowering my daughters with all that I now know."

You too will become more confident after reading this book. That is my promise to you.

You will grow in your awareness of the language you use, both to others and to yourself. You will learn how to reframe what you say and think. And you will be amazed by the impact this has on your confidence and how much more you can achieve.

To help you get there, this book is written in three parts.

In Part One you will learn:

- Why we keep apologising.
- That you are not alone.
- Who your inner critic is and what they are saying to you.

- That your inner critic has one job.
- That you can choose to listen to your inner cheerleader.

Part Two tells you a selection of stories about apologising and confidence that give you tangible and practical tools you can start using immediately.

Finally, Part Three gives you the opportunity to think about what's next for you and what your commitments are. You will build a plan to help you achieve all you want.

My hope is that when you put this book down, you feel a surge in confidence to move out of your comfort zone. You can ask for that pay rise or finally start that business. You can prioritise what you care about and build habits you can stick to. You know what matters most to you and you can boldly take action to move towards it. I hope you will feel that surge in confidence to be authentically you.

YOU'RE INVITED!

This is your invitation to get a pen and scribble all over this book as you read it. I know that may freak you out. But try it, just this once! If you are listening to this book or reading an eBook, have a notepad nearby or create a new note on your phone to help you think about *you* as you go.

- Write down what resonates for *you*.
- Think about and write down how you can apply what you read to *you*.
- Underline the elements that inspire *you*.
- At the end of each chapter add your takeaways to my summary.

Check out the free online book resources to help you get the most from this book. You can download them at: https://www.tararulecoaching.com/book-downloads.

I'll guide you at the perfect time to check them out.

There is space in this book for you to reflect on many of the questions. Write sentences, use bullet points, draw a picture or create a mind map. Do whatever feels good to you. If you write something, you're five times more likely to remember it. I'd love you to remember all the juicy bits that resonate with you so you can put them into action to stop apologising, silence your inner critic, find your confidence and stop saying sorry.

When you do get to those juicy bits that stop you in your tracks, please let me know so I can see the ripple effect this book is creating. Get in contact and share on your socials, tagging me @tararulecoaching.

This book has been written to challenge you so you're not *just* inspired but so you put what you learn into action and stop saying sorry. Don't skim through it. Take the time you deserve to absorb, reflect and answer the questions.

You will be asked deep questions, some of which you may find challenging. This is on purpose. To truly silence your inner critic, find your confidence and stop saying sorry once and for all, you'll need to dig deep, reflect, think about yourself and decide what you want to do differently.

You will have the opportunity to challenge and change some deep-rooted beliefs. This can feel like you're changing who you are and you may find moments emotionally challenging. When I went through this journey myself, I had to process memories I found upsetting and you might do that too.

However, know that you are safe and exactly where you are meant to be right now. You can apply some lightbulb moments and tools straight away, while others will take longer and require more practice. I ask you to be kind to yourself as you go.

In my workshops, people have the opportunity to learn, reflect and apply so that the impact is as great as possible. I invite you to learn, reflect and apply throughout this book too. Learn why you do what you do and how you can grow. Take time to reflect on what applies to you and your life and apply the tools you learn along the way.

Go on… be indulgent. Take the time to think about yourself, not about the job, the kids, the responsibilities, the house or the never-ending to do list. Every time you pick up this book or press play, come to it with openness and kindness.

Get ready to use this as an opportunity to understand yourself more. The more you understand *you* – what you're good at, what you tell yourself, what drives you, what you want – the happier and more successful you'll be.

Make sure you tell your friends and colleagues about this book so that together we can impact even more people.

Now it is time to turn the page and start your journey.

PART ONE

YOUR APOLOGISING RULES

Perhaps you are excited to learn about yourself. Maybe you're excited to learn some new tools. Are you excited thinking about your future, a future in which you're more assertive? When I start a new book, I'm often excited to see how much I already know and do, how much I know in theory but don't actually apply and how much is completely new to me.

You have picked up or downloaded this book because you're aware that you apologise too much and wish you didn't. You will learn how to switch from feeling the need to say sorry all the time to feeling more confident and sounding more assertive. You will be introduced to tools you can put into practice immediately.

Don't get me wrong: I'm not saying you should never apologise or be rude all the time; be aware of the times you say sorry and question if you need to.

It's all very well to tell you to stop apologising, but you may feel overwhelmed by *how* to do it! To help you, I've built some simple RULES so you can create Your Rule Book™.

You can head to the book resources page at: https://www.tararulecoaching.com/book-downloads to download a PDF of Your Apologising Rules.

Your Apologising Rules are:

Realise why.
Unpick it.
Listen to your inner cheerleader.
Establish your toolbox.
Start *now*.

Let's take a moment to break each of these down.

Realise why. Why do you apologise? It is one thing to know you do it, but it is hard to change unless you know why. It could be a habit; it could be due to feedback you received years ago or how you were brought up. Figuring out why you do it is the first step.

Unpick it. What are you telling yourself? When you dig a little deeper, you'll often find that you're telling yourself something that results in you apologising. Perhaps you are telling yourself you don't deserve a seat at the table, that other people are more important than you or you want everyone to like you.

Listen to your inner cheerleader. What is your truth? Throughout this book, you will meet your inner critic and understand what they are saying to you. But you will also meet your inner cheerleader. They have a voice too, even if they're really quiet. What are they trying to tell you?

Establish your toolbox. In Part Two you will explore tools that help you stop apologising. You can choose to apply the ones that fit you and your life best to create Your Rule Book™.

*Start **now**.* How many times do you hear something inspiring: a tip, a tool or a quote and you think, *yes!* Then three weeks pass and you completely forget it. I challenge you to start now! Don't even wait until you finish this book. You can start straight away.

"THE ONLY WAY TO GET BETTER AT PRESS UPS IS TO START!"

- attributed to fitness and motivational speaker, Tim Fargo

I love this quote because it is so true and so applicable to many things in life. The only way you will stop apologising is to start. Take steps now. Do not tell yourself you can't stop. Do not wait to be perfect. As you read, think about what you can put into practice straight away.

1
WHY WE KEEP APOLOGISING

Let's start at the beginning…

Why do we keep apologising? Why are *you* apologising? What makes you feel you should or need to apologise?

There is an excellent reason for 'Realise Why' to be the first step of Your Apologising Rules. When you understand yourself better, when you know your triggers, when you know why you keep saying sorry, you can choose whether you want to carry on doing and believing it or to do something different. The more you know *you*, the happier and more successful you'll be.

Have you heard children saying, "Why? Why? Why?" over and over again? Children ask 'why' all the time! If you are a parent, have you ever put your head in your hands when your child asks, "Why?" for the hundredth time? Children are naturally inquisitive. It is how we learn. It is how we understand the world. It is how we grow. It is how we learn right from wrong.

As we get older, we are taught to stop asking questions. We are told to just get on and do whatever the adult is telling us to do. Some people reach adulthood still full of curiosity, but others stop asking why. Think like a child. Stop just *doing* and start asking *why*. Get curious, get interested and find your answers.

Start by asking why you apologise.

It could be that it is a habit. Perhaps you got some feedback once that you were too confrontational, aggressive or direct. Maybe you don't feel you belong in the room. Do you think the person you're talking to is smarter or better than you? Or were you taught as a child to apologise?

This issue can particularly affect women. I've heard many more unnecessary apologies from my female colleagues than male ones. Here are some of the reasons why.

1. From a young age, girls tend to be encouraged to avoid conflict and 'play nicely', while boys are more often encouraged to assert themselves and be more independent.
2. Women are often more empathetic which can sound apologetic in the way they communicate.
3. When a woman asserts herself at work, especially in male-dominated environments, she can feel she is going against expectations so softens her language to compensate and avoid conflict.

While all this is true, I want to be clear that this book isn't written only for women, it is for everyone because so many people apologise too much and lack confidence regardless of gender. I am telling you why women apologise more than men because I don't want you to beat yourself up if you are female and you see that you apologise more than your husband, partner or male colleagues and friends. Be kind to yourself.

SO WHY DO YOU APOLOGISE?

When I qualified as a professional coach back in 2018, one of the first things I remember being taught was: Don't ask why. When we hear the word why, we automatically feel we are being judged. Even if the question is asked with positive intent, we have an emotional reaction to the word. So instead, most of my coaching questions start with 'what', 'how' or 'who'.

I don't think it's always correct, though. Sometimes we need to ask why in order to get to the root of the problem and understand ourselves better. Therefore, I ask you why you apologise? Allow your thoughts to come without any judgement. Be kind to yourself.

I hear many people talk to themselves in a way they never would to someone else. Instead, talk to yourself as if you were talking to your best friend. If you are surprised by things that come up, good! You are developing a deeper understanding of yourself. Try to hold off judgement of yourself.

Let's take the next step. Under each question that follows you have space to write down your thoughts. Write bullet points, draw something, do a mind map or write full sentences, whatever feels good to you.

Reading an eBook? Grab your notebook now. If you're listening to this on audiobook, allow yourself to pause after each question so you can think and reflect and write down what comes up for you.

To help you think about *why*, let's start with *when*. When do you notice that you apologise?

Do you apologise in meetings? When you send messages? In emails? During everyday conversations? When you bump into a stranger? When someone bumps into you? When you remind a waiter that you ordered your drinks thirty minutes ago? When you ask for something?

Perhaps it is not only when you say the word 'sorry'. Do you also diminish what you say when you make a very good point by ending it with a round-about apology like, "That's just my opinion." Do you belittle your own statements in this way?

Maybe your way of apologising is by saying nothing at all. You have an idea but instead of speaking up, you sit there quietly.

— **When do you apologise?**

Who do you apologise to?

Your boss? Your friends? Peers? People who are more senior than you? All your colleagues? Particular colleagues? Your partner? Your family? Specific friends? Strangers?

— **Who do you apologise to?**

What do you notice when you reflect on when you apologise and who to?

Do you apologise more in front of a certain person, or with people of a particular seniority or level? Does the size of the audience make a difference? Is it when you feel triggered? Are you more likely to apologise in certain situations? Does it feel like you say sorry all the time, to everyone?

— **What do you notice?**

What makes you feel you *should* apologise?

Is there already a story you can sense you're telling yourself… that you don't belong, that you're not good enough, that other people are more important? Does it feel like a habit you don't know how to crack? (Yet!) Is it something you learnt to do as a child? Did you get some feedback that still hurts?

— **What makes you feel like you *should* apologise?**

Reflecting on the when, the who, the what and your feelings.

— **Why do you think you apologise?**

You may have found that easy, you may have found it hard or you may still be thinking. Remember, resist the urge to judge yourself. Some of my clients know instantly why they apologise and others need longer to reflect.

If you're not quite sure about why you apologise, mark this page so you can come back to it later, or write the question down if you're listening on audiobook or reading an eBook.

HABITS

Habit forming
(*verb*)
doing the same thing repeatedly, until it becomes automatic and you no longer have to think about it.

~~~~~~~~~~~~~~~~

Habits can be great. Getting into the habit of cleaning your teeth twice a day, drinking a glass of water first thing, thinking of what you're grateful for as soon as you wake up or stretching while cleaning your teeth (maybe that's just me, though!) are all great habits you can form.

People often tell me they apologise out of habit. Was this part of your why?

However, not all habits are ones we would choose if we consciously thought about them.

A BIT OF SCIENCE

Did you know that you have sixty thousand thoughts a day? Ninety-five percent of them are in your subconscious. That means you are not even consciously thinking about most of what you do, from breathing and blinking to swallowing your saliva. They just happen, thanks to your subconscious. This is great news. Imagine how much noise there would be in your brain if you were reading this book while also thinking about breathing, blinking and swallowing your saliva!

However, because your subconscious is so powerful, it also drives thoughts and actions you wouldn't consciously choose, including continuing habits that were formed years ago. That might be writing emails that say thank you one hundred times, believing you are not good enough… or saying sorry all the time. So much is driven by your subconscious.

While we appreciate how amazing our subconscious is because we don't need to think about breathing, it is not so great if it makes you apologise all the time.

THE WHY BEHIND YOUR HABIT?

I used to work with someone – let's call her Maria – who apologised in meetings a lot. We spoke about it, and her first reaction when we started digging into her why was that it was just a habit. She would say it without thinking.

We could have left it there and written it off as a habit that was hard to change. However, we dug a bit deeper and she said, "But everyone else in the room is so smart. I feel lower than them all and that I don't really deserve to be there."

That, right there, was her why. Yes, it was a habit, but one formed due to her beliefs that she didn't deserve to be there. That was why she apologised for it.

If one of your reasons for apologising is that it is a habit, reflect a little longer on why that habit started in the first place. What belief sits underneath the habit? Once you know your why, it is much easier to choose something different.

— What is the why behind your habit?

WHY WE KEEP APOLOGISING

PART OF YOUR IDENTITY

Do you feel that apologising has become part of your identity? That it is not just something you do, but who you are?

When I was interviewing people for this book, one lady told me, "I'm an apologiser." She did not say she apologises too much or she has a habit of apologising, but that *she is* an apologiser. It had become part of her identity.

She said she spots that her mum apologises all the time, and it is a learnt behaviour of hers too. Because she says sorry all the time, the words 'I'm sorry' have lost their meaning in their house. She now hears her own kids apologising. However, her kids say it flippantly, without actually meaning it.

How about you? Can you see who you learnt it from? Are you teaching those around you to apologise too? What's the impact on your loved ones when you say sorry too much? Do you cook your partner a meal and say sorry straight away? Sorry it's late, sorry it's not amazing or sorry it's not something original?

Perhaps you have children and you hear them apologising when they don't need to. Do they apologise when they ask you for something, or when you give them something? How could this impact them in the future? Or has the word sorry lost all meaning for them? Do they accidentally hurt someone and then say sorry without meaning it? Do they say sorry, but when you ask them what they're sorry for, they have no idea?

How about at work? When you apologise for asking a question, apologise for interrupting, or apologise for taking up someone's time, how do you come across? Do you come across as confident and strong or weak and insecure? Are you giving your power away?

Does it feel like other people are taking your power? You are giving your power to them. They are not doing anything; it is you, when you apologise, giving it away.

Let's look at a couple of examples.

You are in a meeting and someone is presenting. They are quite sure of themselves but have made a point you don't understand, have skimmed over a really important area, or you have another idea that could help.

You say, "Sorry, this may be a stupid question but…" It may be a habit, you may not be aware you're saying it, or in that moment you may be thinking that you do feel stupid because everyone else already knows the answer.

Take a moment to think about the presenter's thoughts. Also, what do all the other people in the room think?

Do they think, "Ooh, I can't wait to hear this question; it will probably be really insightful." Or do they think, "I'm bored already! Why do people ask stupid questions? Hurry up so we can move on!"

The latter is far more likely because you have just told them (and their subconscious) you're asking a stupid question. You may have said it without meaning it. You may have said it as a joke. But their subconscious doesn't know that! Their subconscious has just been given very clear direction: they are about to be asked a stupid question.

You're wrapping your power up in a bow, passing it across the table and saying, "What I'm about to say isn't very smart, interesting or important so please feel free to ignore me." They may reassure you or take pity on you but you're not after their pity!

How about this one: you start a conversation with, "Sorry for taking up your time."

Do they think, "We are about to have a really juicy conversation here. Let me pay full attention and see what they want to talk about."

Or do they think, "Don't they know how busy I am? Let's make this quick because I'm important and I've got so much to do!"

Again, you are planting a seed into their subconscious that they don't need to pay attention to what you say, even if they like and respect you. Remember, ninety-five percent of their thoughts are driven by their subconscious. What you plant is so important.

— **When you apologise, what do you believe other people think?**

THE IMPACT

Apologising too much has an impact on you in various ways.

When you apologise for asking a stupid question, colleagues are less likely to listen to you. You are less likely to get that pay rise because you're too busy apologising for taking up your boss's time to confidently ask for what you want. You are less likely to influence others' actions and this causes you frustration, but on reflection, this is unsurprising since your opening sentence was an apology.

At home, you try to do it all and feel stressed. You would have too many apologies to make if you, heaven forbid, put yourself first! Do you ever feel guilty for prioritising you?

— **What is the impact from apologising too much?**

Know that it is ok to stop apologising, even if you feel that it is a core part of your identity. You have permission to stop saying sorry and to feel more confident.

SUMMARY - WHY WE KEEP APOLOGISING

- Get curious, think like a child and ask yourself why.
- 'Realise Why' is the first step to creating Your Apologising Rules because it is much easier to change when you understand why.
- Be kind to yourself; don't judge yourself while you're thinking about your why. Talk to yourself as if you were talking to your best friend.
- Reflect on when you apologise and who you apologise to. What do you notice and what makes you feel you *should* apologise?
- Ninety-five percent of your thoughts are driven by your subconscious.
- Your subconscious is amazingly powerful. Try to become aware of the thoughts and actions you have not been consciously aware of.
- What beliefs sit behind your habits?
- The more you understand yourself, the happier and more successful you'll be.
- When you apologise but don't need to, you're giving away your power.

REFLECT

Take a moment to pause and write down your answers to these three questions.

— **When do you find yourself apologising?**

— What is the why behind your habits?

— Why do you think you apologise?

What else do you want to remember from this chapter?

2
YOU ARE NOT THE ONLY ONE

YOU ARE NOT ALONE!

You have spent time thinking about why you apologise, and perhaps you have already learnt something new about yourself – maybe about how you talk to yourself or why your habit of saying sorry started.

Sometimes people at this stage think they are the only ones talking to themselves like this. The only one who can't crack the habit of apologising. The only one acting in a certain way because of something that happened years ago. Perhaps you are beating yourself up right now. Please don't.

Emotions are deeply personal so it can feel isolating to work through them. That is, we can each believe we are alone in feeling this way. You are not alone.

You would be amazed how many people I coach think they're the only ones who…

- Think they're not good enough.
- Wish they were more confident.
- Do not have life sorted.
- Do not know what to do next with their lives.
- Feel stupid.
- Think they have to be perfect.

The reality is that they are not alone and neither are you. So many people I talk to have the exact same challenges. Plus, there are lots of points on the list above that have struck a chord with me over the years.

COMPARISON IS A JOY KILLER

Social media dominates many of our lives. We see people living the 'perfect life'. Everyone 'has it all' and is 'doing it all'; everyone is #LivingMyBestLife! But not everyone shares real life.

While I wish everyone *was* living their perfect life (I really do wish more of the world felt happier) it is often smoke and mirrors, and comparing ourselves to others brings us down even more. Unfortunately, not many people feel upbeat after scrolling for half an hour on social media, because subconsciously we compare ourselves with what others look like, what they're doing and what they're saying.

Everyone has their challenges. No one is perfect.

"WE COMPARE THE BEST OF OTHERS AGAINST THE WORST OF OURSELVES"

- *Eric Thomas*

I can illustrate this with myself as an example.

I am quite open with people and am happy to be vulnerable. I tell people how I sabotage myself, what my inner critic says to me and I share tips on how to balance life when you feel like you're juggling everything. But still, the question people ask me most often is, "How do you do it all?"

By *all* they mean have a successful career, run my own business and bring up two girls with a smile on my face. (Most of the time!) I used to feel a funny kind of pride that people thought I was doing it all, when I didn't feel like I was in the slightest. But then I realised it was a lie!

I am honest with people now and say, "I don't do it all! I'm constantly prioritising. I know what I'm good at and what gives me energy, and I spend time doing those things. I'm constantly challenging myself to grow and develop. I outsource or delegate as much as I can. At no point am I doing it all!"

Please let this sink in. I am not doing it all. No one is. Just like no one is perfect and no one is confident all the time.

Think about what you love doing or what you're good at and spend as much time as possible doing those things. What don't you enjoy? What aren't you good at? Who can you ask to help? What can you outsource? What can you delegate to others? You may not enjoy doing something but it will be someone else's strength.

BUT THEY KNOW EVERYTHING!

The other week one of my clients compared herself to one of her colleagues. She said, "But she knows *everything* and she's *always* confident." She was beating herself up for what she thought she lacked.

This is called cognitive distortion, when we exaggerate, over-generalise, jump to conclusions or have an all-or-nothing view. It is perfectly normal.

My client and I started to dig, and she soon realised what she said wasn't true. She knew her colleague got nervous when she was asked to talk on stage, so she wasn't confident all the time. Her colleague didn't know everything, she just spoke confidently about what she did know, asked questions and played to her strengths. No one knows *everything*! Even ChatGPT doesn't know anything beyond January 2022 at the time of writing in 2024.

No one is *always* confident. You grow in confidence by knowing who you are and what you're good at and showing up as the unique and brilliant you.

"BE YOURSELF; EVERYONE ELSE IS TAKEN."

- Oscar Wilde

When I have told people the title of the book I have been writing, an astonishing number have said, "Wow, I need to read that book." You are not the only one who is apologising, not feeling confident, feeling stressed, feeling not good enough, feeling you need to be perfect feeling like you have the weight of the world on your shoulders. We are often our own biggest critics.

What do you want to remind yourself? It could be that you are not alone, you don't have to do it all, social media isn't a true reflection of real life, no one knows everything, or no one is confident all the time.

— **What do you want to remind yourself?**

If you left the question blank in the last chapter about why you keep apologising, are you ready to go back now and reflect?

SUMMARY - YOU'RE NOT THE ONLY ONE

- You are not the only one who apologises too much, doesn't feel confident and says horrible things to themselves.
- We compare the best of others with the worst of ourselves.
- No one is doing it all (including me).
- No one is assertive all the time (including me).
- No one is confident all the time (including me).
- No one knows everything (including me and ChatGPT).
- Be yourself and be kind to yourself.
- You are taking the right steps to stop apologising, silence your inner critic and find your confidence.

REFLECT

Take a moment to pause and write down what came up for you in this chapter. What do you want to remind yourself?

3

LET ME INTRODUCE YOU TO DOBBY

UNPICK IT

Let's dig deeper to help you understand the stories you're telling yourself and meet your inner critic.

In Your Apologising Rules, your second step is to 'Unpick It', to dig deeper and understand the stories you're telling yourself which lead to you apologise and feel that lack of confidence. You will meet your inner critic so you can start to silence it and choose something different.

This is a powerful step. You may start by thinking about what your inner critic is telling you which means you apologise, but you will probably go so much deeper than this. You will probably discover a story that impacts your overall confidence.

TIME TO MEET DOBBY!

People often find it helpful to personify their inner critic as a character, perhaps one from a book or a film. For me, it is Dobby the house elf from JK Rowling's *Harry Potter*. He is three feet tall with bat-like ears and bulging green eyes. He talks about himself in the third person and works for a family who aren't very nice. Every time he is mean about his 'master' he hurts himself saying, "Bad Dobby, very bad Dobby!"

I have a voice in my head, my inner critic, and he looks like Dobby. Every time I'm nice about myself I picture him head-butting the wall and saying, "Bad Dobby, can't be nice about yourself! Very bad Dobby!"

Inner critic
(noun)
the negative voice in your head saying you can't do something or you aren't good enough because it's driven by fear.

~~~~~~~~~~

Why does he say I can't be nice about myself? He has a belief… *I* have a belief that I'm not good enough.

Everyone has an inner critic. They're the voice in your head saying you're not good enough, not smart enough, you have to be perfect, and you are going to be judged.

For me, I can see what my inner critic is doing. For you, maybe you can hear a shrill voice, smell a certain perfume, feel it in the pit of your stomach. You may already know what yours says to you. Don't worry if you don't yet as you'll get an opportunity to reflect in a few minutes.

— What is your inner critic telling you?

— What do they look like or sound like?

BELIEFS

What do you believe? This may sound like a strange question, but we don't often stop to consider and be conscious of our beliefs. Your beliefs are incredibly powerful and drive so many of your actions. They are formed by the stories you tell yourself, your experiences and things you hear other people say.

What others say → Your beliefs → Your actions
Stories you tell yourself →
Your experiences →

However, beliefs are not facts. We rarely stop and get curious about our beliefs in order to challenge them.

"A BELIEF IS JUST A STORY YOU'VE TOLD YOURSELF THOUSANDS OF TIMES."

- Linda Raschke

Some of the following examples might reflect your own actions as driven by your beliefs.

- You treat other people with respect because you believe you're a good person.
- You give to charity because you believe you should give back if you're able to.
- You push for equality because you believe it is right and fair.

These are all great. Let's take it one step further.

- You don't want to give a presentation on stage because you believe you may make a fool of yourself.
- You apologise for taking up someone's time because you believe their time is more precious than yours.
- You say sorry for asking a stupid question because you believe you're not that smart.

LET ME INTRODUCE YOU TO DOBBY

But where did those beliefs come from?

- Perhaps your belief that you'll make a fool of yourself came from your parents telling you this.
- Did your belief that another person's time is more precious than yours come from an old boss's feedback that you took up too much of their time?
- If you believe you're not smart enough, did a teacher once make you feel stupid?

The actions you take every single day are driven by your beliefs. When did you last think about where those beliefs came from, let alone challenge them?

Many of your beliefs were formed when you were young, so you may not even be aware of them. Before age seven, your brain is like a sponge. It takes everything it hears as fact. It doesn't challenge at all. This is why you can tell a young child that the moon is made of cheese and they'll say, "Wow! That's so cool," instead of calling you out for lying.

Although this can seem funny, how many other things did you hear when you were young that your brain soaked up without challenging?

Perhaps you heard that money doesn't grow on trees and now you have a scarcity mindset when it comes to money, driven by that belief implanted years ago. Maybe you heard that you should be seen and not heard so now you'd rather stay quiet in a meeting than voice your opinion. Did you hear that you are bossy? Now you apologise if you ask for anything so others don't think you're bossy.

These comments we hear as children are powerful. They turn into stories we tell ourselves over and over again. They form that little voice in your head telling you not to do something, that you need to keep quiet, that you're not good enough. They become deep-rooted beliefs.

DO YOU WANT TO BE A BULLY?

Your subconscious is amazingly powerful. It operates without you having to think about it; you are not conscious of what it thinks and believes.

Take a few minutes to tune into it, to listen to that subconscious. What is it saying to you? What story is your subconscious telling you? More specifically, what are you telling yourself because you heard someone else say it to you? It wasn't even your thought in the first place, but you heard it (often a long time ago) and it has grown into a belief that you now take as fact.

Perhaps you heard stories as a child that you now realise you have come to believe too, like, "You have to work hard to earn lots of money," or, "You should always respect your elders."

Maybe you saw something when you were growing up that you now believe. Was your dad successful but worked every weekend so you now have a belief that to be successful you have to sacrifice family time or your weekends?

For years I had a belief that to be a top leader you have to be a bully. Why? Because I had evidence! I had seen it! I knew two people whose leadership style I didn't agree with. I saw them as bullies and my subconscious made up a story that you have to be a bully to be a leader.

It wasn't until I was coached many years later that I recognised this belief. Before the coaching, I would say that I didn't want to be too successful, I definitely never wanted to reach CEO level and I was quite happy at the level I was at. Why would I ever push for a promotion or have huge career aspirations when my subconscious believed that I'd have to become a bully? When my coach helped me dig a bit deeper, I became aware of this story that was holding me back.

Hearing this, what stories are you telling yourself?

— **What have you seen or heard that could be holding you back?**

Once I realised how much I was limiting my career aspirations due to just two people and that I knew many successful leaders who weren't bullies, I began to dream bigger, to realise it was *ok* to want to progress more, it was *ok* to want to be a CEO. And now I'm the CEO and Founder of my own business! I dread to think where I'd be now if I hadn't tuned into that belief and kept on believing that successful leaders are all bullies.

WHAT'S STOPPING YOU?

I run a great workshop called 'What's Stopping You?' to help people realise the stories their inner critic is telling them, the impact it has and what their inner cheerleader wants to remind them of. I have run it with graduates, women's networks, leaders, whole teams and charities across the world.

And do you know what? *Everyone* connects with the idea of having an inner critic, regardless of gender, age or background. An inner critic isn't heard by a select few. I am yet to meet someone who says, "I've no idea what you're talking about. I've never felt scared or doubted myself."

Some people's inner critic is really loud and jumps up and down and shouts all day long. For some, it only pops up now and then. For others it is quiet most of the time. But we all have one. It is in our heads telling us stories, reinforcing our beliefs.

How about your inner critic?

- **Is your inner critic there occasionally or all the time? Is it loud or quiet?**

IMPOSTER SYNDROME

You may have heard the term imposter syndrome to describe this. It is more or less synonymous but I find people tend to use the term *inner critic* more readily. Most people can apply it to themselves.

Imposter syndrome
(noun)
feeling inadequate, doubting your accomplishments; a fear of being found out despite being competent and successful.

The first time I heard the phrase *imposter syndrome*, I was lying on a sun lounger in Tenerife. Instead of a light hearted romance, I was reading *The Secret Thoughts of Successful Women* by Valerie Young. I was shocked how much it resonated with me. I learnt that people with imposter syndrome tend to credit external factors and luck rather than owning their accomplishments. You can feel like a fraud and believe you'll be found out any time and it will all come crashing down. You are driven by perfectionism, fear of failure and comparing yourself with others. While reading, I was thinking, "Yes, yes, yes!"

It was the first time I realised how much I told people I was lucky instead of owning my successes. I dismissed compliments all the time. I loved putting pressure on myself to hit a deadline. I had high expectations of others, but even higher expectations of myself and I realised that deep down, I didn't think I was good enough. It was a powerful book!

When I came home, I told my boss about it. I said, "I've learnt about imposter syndrome and I think I have it, but what if I don't have it? What if I'm actually rubbish at my job!" I think she may have put her head in her hands at that point. To put it into perspective, I was already a Director in a huge global company. I wasn't rubbish at my job.

YOU'RE JUST LUCKY!

One of the stories my inner critic, Dobby, has told me over and over again through the years is that I'm just lucky.

If I got a pay rise, I thought I was lucky. When I got a promotion, I told everyone I was lucky. When I was offered a job at a different company, I said I was lucky the interviewer liked me. If a presentation went well, I said I was lucky as people had gone easy on me.

Over and over again, I said, "I'm lucky," and whenever someone paid me a compliment, I batted it away and told them I was just lucky. Do you dismiss compliments too?

A boss once told me, when someone gives you a compliment, imagine they have gone out and bought you a present; they are giving you a gift wrapped in a bow. You wouldn't say, "Oh no, I don't deserve this," and throw it aside without opening it. There is only one suitable response, and that is, "Thank you." She challenged me to only ever say thank you when I receive a compliment, and I challenge you to do the same.

Now, it feels so much better to smile and say, "Thank you," than to give an excuse as to why I don't deserve the compliment. Plus, I'm sure they feel better that I'm not throwing their compliment away by dismissing it.

Accounting for everything by calling it luck was a story I was telling myself. Four years ago, I realised how deep this feeling of not being good enough was when my coach helped me understand where it came from. I grew up in an area where we had something called a 12 plus. At age twelve, everyone took an exam to see what school we would go to next. We would either pass and go to a grammar school, or we wouldn't and go to a secondary school.

I still remember being on the school playground to pick up my results. They were given to us in big white envelopes. All my friends opened theirs and one by one I heard an excited scream as they found out they'd passed. I chose not to open my envelope. I walked away from the school gates with my mum, and eventually I stopped to open it.

When I told my coach this story, I said that I opened the envelope and it said, "You're not good enough." Then, right then in that moment, my twelve-year-old self formed a belief that I wasn't good enough. I realise now that the letter didn't say, "You're not good enough," it just said a score which was lower than the pass mark, but in my brain, I overwrote what it actually said with the words, "You're not good enough."

The funny thing is that I've had lots of successes since then. I did great in my GCSEs, the exams you do at age sixteen. But I told myself I was so lucky to get good results despite 'failing' my 12 plus. I went on and did A-levels (more exams) when I was eighteen and got relatively good results. I felt so lucky that I got to take them as not many people at my school did. A pattern started. I worked hard, got a good result and credited luck!

Fast forward another twenty years and I realised that I often procrastinated when it came to doing big presentations. I always left them to the last minute. Deep down my inner critic thought I wasn't good enough and didn't want to be proved right. If I prepared a presentation a week in advance and it went badly... well, that would prove I wasn't good enough. But if I left it to the last minute and it went badly, I could blame it on the fact that I only had one day to prepare. Much better that than my inner critic being proved right!

When I realised this, I was blown away. My inner critic was so scared that it was sabotaging me.

The funny thing is, none of my presentations were a failure. Every single one went well. I look back now and wonder just how amazing they could have been if I hadn't been driven by fear, if I had allowed myself to prepare them a week early rather than the night before.

I was almost forty when I realised how strong this story and belief was. Since properly unpicking it and unlocking it, I can honestly say that my whole life has completely changed.

What sounds similar to your experience? Is there an excuse you tend to give yourself if you do well? Has this prompted a childhood memory? Do you find yourself procrastinating? What actions do you take day to day that on reflection don't help you?

YOU'RE NOT AN ENTREPRENEUR!

More recently, I noticed my inner critic telling me the story that I am not an entrepreneur.

I have coached people formally and informally for years. It started as informal chats with the new graduates at O2 where I worked ten years ago. Someone would see me in the coffee queue and stop me to ask for advice. It progressed to mentoring and more formal conversations. When I qualified as a professional coach I realised the difference between mentoring – when you give advice – and coaching when you ask questions and help people find their own answers.

I realised coaching gave me so much energy. I spent as much time as possible coaching while also doing my big corporate job. Over and over again when I coached people or talked about coaching people said to me, "You're an amazing coach. Would you ever leave and do coaching?" My response over and over again was, "No, I'm not an entrepreneur, but maybe one day I'll have earned enough money in corporate so I can leave and do a bit of coaching."

I must have told this story hundreds of times, until one day, a couple of years ago, I suddenly heard myself and realised what I was doing. I was telling anyone who would listen, anyone who thought I was a great coach, anyone who encouraged me, that I was not an entrepreneur!

This story, this belief was having a huge impact on my life. It was stopping me from taking the leap of faith in myself, from setting up my own business to do something I loved and was great at because I was so scared of failing. My actions (or inaction) were linked all the way back to me feeling like I wasn't good enough and triggering my twelve-year-old emotions.

But it wasn't me saying that. It was my inner critic. I think I may have actually laughed out loud when I realised. I remember messaging my work bestie from the sofa at home to tell her the story I had identified.

She replied instantly. "What do you mean?" she said. "You are an entrepreneur. Check out this article." I looked through the article she'd sent on the top qualities of an entrepreneur.

- Good decision-maker. Check.
- Financial acumen. Check.
- Networking skills. Check.
- Proactive. Check.

The list went on. Check. Check. Check!

There was only one to which I didn't immediately say, "Check!" and that was being creative. With hindsight, I know I am creative, but again, my inner critic was comparing my creativity with that of my colleagues and at the time I worked at a creative software company! If I read that article again, I would be kinder to myself, listen to my inner cheerleader and give creativity a "Check!" too.

I now had some evidence to prove my inner critic wrong. It wasn't true that I was not an entrepreneur. I wasn't quite ready to say, "I am an entrepreneur," but I was happy to never again say I wasn't one. I started saying, "I have loads of entrepreneurial qualities."

This tiny but important shift in my belief unlocked so much. There is no way I'd have been as successful as I am now, as the CEO and Founder of my own business, if I still believed I was not an entrepreneur.

Three months after this realisation, I was at a coaching retreat. I said for the first time ever, "I am an entrepreneur." The reaction from my coaches and the other amazing ladies in the room was immense. I felt so much love and it felt so powerful to believe in myself.

Another three months on, I said for the first time, "I am a successful entrepreneur." I still remember that huge moment. I became immediately excited about all the possibilities for me and my business.

LET'S MEET YOUR INNER CRITIC

You have now heard a few things my inner critic has told me over the years. It is time for you to reflect on the story your inner critic is telling you, what it is stopping you from doing, what it looks, sounds or feels like and what it is called.

One of the purposes of this book is to help you to silence your inner critic. The best way to do that is by listening to it, leaning all the way in and hearing what it has to say so that it feels safe enough to start being quieter. When your critic is quieter, this gives you the opportunity to listen to your inner cheerleader more.

Consider first what your inner critic is telling you. Perhaps you're telling yourself you don't deserve a seat at the table, other people are more important than you, you need to be seen and not heard or you need everyone to like you. Are you telling yourself you're not good enough, you're not an entrepreneur, you're not a leader, you're not smart enough? Maybe you're saying you don't deserve this, you need to be grateful, you're too old or you're too young.

Tune into your inner critic. Listen to them. What are they saying to you?

LET ME INTRODUCE YOU TO DOBBY

— **What is your inner critic telling you?**

What's the impact on you of repeatedly listening to this inner critic of yours?

Maybe it stops you being assertive, talking up in meetings, starting your own business, asking for a pay rise, going for a new role, preparing presentations in advance, asking questions, or stretching out of your comfort zone.

— **What is it stopping you from doing?**

Remember, this is a process and a journey. You may have found it easy to reflect on your inner critic or you may have found it hard. You may have written lots or one thing. Wherever you are, it is ok. You are doing the work to figure this stuff out and I am proud of you. I hope you're proud of yourself too.

When you think about your inner critic, does an image or a name pop into your mind? What does your inner critic look like, sound like or feel like? Mine is like Dobby from *Harry Potter*, remember, headbutting the wall when I am nice to myself.

Some of my clients have said their inner critic talks in a high-pitched voice and is tall and thin. Another doesn't have an image but they speak in a stern voice like their dad's. One feels theirs in the pit of their stomach, and another smells the perfume it wears.

Below is space for you to reflect. You may want to doodle and draw an image. Feel free to label what you see. You can write down bullet points of what you notice or do a mind map. Feel free to get creative, even if your inner critic tells you you're not very creative.

If your inner critic resembles your parents, that is ok and also perfectly normal. It doesn't mean you need to tell them, but I would invite you to believe that they were doing the best they could with the information they had at the time.

Just like earlier when you were digging into your why, come to this with no judgement. Take time to get closer to your inner critic for a moment so you can choose whether you keep listening or not.

- **What does your inner critic look like, sound like or feel like? Do they have a name?**

YOUR INNER CHEERLEADER IS THERE TOO

Let's take a moment to meet someone else: your inner cheerleader.

Yes, we all have an inner critic, but we all have an inner cheerleader too. They may be really quiet and you may not have heard them in a while, but they're there, I promise you. In a couple of chapters, you will tune into what they have to say but just know for now that they exist.

Inner cheerleader
(noun)
the kind and
comforting voice
in your head who
speaks the truth, who
knows you can do
it and is driven by
positivity, possibility
and hope.

My inner cheerleader is a warm comforting feeling rather than a distinct character. I often refer to them as she, but because I'm so used to tuning into my inner cheerleader, it is often Dobby himself who picks up the pom poms to cheer me on!

Can you already see, hear or feel your inner cheerleader?

SUMMARY - LET ME INTRODUCE YOU TO DOBBY

- The second step of Your Apologising Rules is to Unpick It. By going a level deeper you are better able to choose something different.
- Your actions are driven by your beliefs.
- Your beliefs are just stories you have told yourself thousands of times.
- Reflect on what you heard or saw as a child that has turned into deep-rooted beliefs.
- Your inner critic is the voice in your head driven by fear.
- Everyone has an inner critic but some are louder than others.
- Your inner critic can give excuses to your successes like "I'm just lucky."
- It believes things like, "I'm not good enough," and, "I'm not an entrepreneur."
- These beliefs and stories can stop you from doing a great deal without you even being aware of them.
- When you think of your inner critic you may have an image, a sound, a feeling or a name come to mind.
- Remember to be kind to yourself.
- You've got an inner cheerleader by your side too.

REFLECT

Take a moment to pause and write down your answers to these three questions.

— **What have you seen or heard through your life that now feels like deep-rooted beliefs?**

— **What is your inner critic telling you?**

— **Are you ready to turn down the volume of your inner critic?**

What else do you want to remember from this chapter?

4

YOU HAD ONE JOB

THE REASON YOUR INNER CRITIC EXISTS

You have spent time getting to know your inner critic, the stories it is telling you and what it is stopping you from doing. But why is it telling you all these things? For what benefit? It is actually quite simple. Your brain has one job, and that is to keep you safe.

It is a protective mechanism. Whether it is rational or not, you have a fear that your brain, your inner critic is trying to keep you safe from. All those beliefs are there to keep you safe.

If you doubt yourself, if you think you're not good enough, if you don't feel confident, if you apologise too much, or if you want to be perfect, it is because your brain has a desire for safety and security.

LET'S TALK ABOUT THE IMPACT

The impact on you and your life of listening to your inner critic and 'staying safe' can be huge. If you tell yourself you're not good enough, not smart enough, or you can't be vulnerable, what's the impact? Are you staying safe by not going for that promotion? Not saying yes to opportunities? Not starting your own business? Not posting on social media? Not speaking up?

— **What's the impact on you of 'staying safe'?**

— **What is it stopping you from doing?**

When these fears lead to you apologising all the time, what is the impact of constantly saying, "Sorry for interrupting!" or, "Sorry, this may be a stupid question," or, "Sorry, I know everyone else knows what's going on but…" or, "Sorry for taking up your time"?

Do colleagues take you less seriously? Are you seen as weak? Do you rarely get what you want? Do you find it hard to influence? Are you indecisive? Do you feel stressed because you feel you can't say no? Do you earn less than you deserve? Is your confidence low? Do you feel drained?

This chapter digs into the science a bit so you can understand how your brain works. Then you'll have the opportunity to think about what your brain, your inner critic is trying to keep you safe from.

A BIT OF SCIENCE

Let's take a brief look at how our brains work. There are lots of great books that can tell you all the details and all the science; I will share with you the summary and highlights from some that I've read.

Your brain consists of three main components: the emotional brain (which includes the amygdala), the rational brain (particularly the prefrontal cortex) and the memory system or computer (often referred to as the database of memories). All three are important and can work together nicely, but they can also experience conflicts at times.

In addition, you also have a conscious and subconscious. Conscious thoughts are those that you are actively aware of and intentionally control, while your subconscious operates below the level of conscious awareness. It involves automatic behaviours and thoughts which are driven by your memories and beliefs, often without you realising why.

YOUR EMOTIONAL BRAIN

Do you ever find yourself thinking or saying something even if you don't truly believe it?

Most of your actions and reactions in the moment are driven by your emotional brain, and this is where your inner critic spends most of its time. In *The Chimp Paradox* (a fabulous book), Professor Steven Peters calls the emotional brain the chimp brain. This part of the brain drives intuition, gut feel and reflexes. It senses fear and its primary job is to keep us safe.

Throughout human evolution, one of the key ways we survived was by being part of a group. This meant we had protection against threats and predators. Fitting in was critical and your emotional brain knew it. If you didn't fit in you could be isolated and kicked out of the pack. Then, quite simply, you had a far lower chance of surviving. It was literally a life-or-death situation to fit in with those around you.

Fast forward through thousands of years of evolution to now, this same need to be part of the pack is still there. It is no longer life or death, but the emotion is still there and as a result, we don't want to stand out, be different, make a fuss or speak up.

It is the reason for groupthink. People choose fitting in and harmony over saying what they really think, often resulting in poor decision-making. We prefer to make a poor decision than stand up to a dominant person or have a different opinion from the rest of the room. The emotional brain wants to be part of the pack.

Your emotional brain is so powerful that not only can it make you keep quiet, but it can also result in you acting completely out of character.

THE EMOTIONAL BRAIN AND ROAD RAGE

The best example to bring this to life is that of road rage. Even thinking about a bad driver cutting you up can raise your blood pressure.

Let's pretend you are driving along when someone cuts in front of you and you have to slam your brakes on. Now, while some people may be unconcerned and carry on as if it never happened, most people experience their emotional brain kicking in.

If you were to listen to your rational brain for a moment it would probably say you shouldn't worry, no one got hurt and it really doesn't matter. But your rational brain doesn't get a chance because your emotional brain is quicker than your rational brain. It has to be quicker because it is there to keep you safe and keep you alive.

Perhaps you mutter something under your breath. Maybe you shout or swear at them. You might feel outraged. How dare they! Your emotional brain is now calling the shots.

THE EMOTIONAL BRAIN AND YOUR SUBCONSCIOUS WORKING TOGETHER

While your emotional brain is extremely powerful, so is your subconscious because it looks to your past experiences to drive automatic behaviour. they often work together to keep you safe.

Let's take the example of standing at the side of the road ready to cross. You don't consciously think about whether you should cross the road now, while that fast car hurtles towards you. You don't rationally ask if you should go now or wait until it has passed. You just wait. You know to wait. But how?

Two things are going on. Your emotional brain is always on the lookout for threats, and the potential threat of the fast car activates a protective response. At the same time, your subconscious brain is looking back to past experiences of fast cars. It knows the threat is high. Together they make an extremely quick assessment and choose to make you stand still and stay alive.

Take a moment to see how amazing your brain is and all the good that comes from your subconscious and your emotional brain.

HERE'S THE BUT!

It is a big but. Your brain tries to keep you safe even when there is no real and present threat.

You do not go for a new role because your subconscious knows there's a chance you may fail. It remembers what it felt like when you failed at age twelve and it never wants you to feel like that again. But remember, you are no longer that twelve-year-old child.

You procrastinate because if you got on and sent that email, wrote that presentation or whatever it is you're putting off, you may do it wrong, it may not be perfect, or it may not be good enough. Your emotional brain wants to keep you safe. Better not do it at all, than show you are not perfect or not good enough. But sending an email that isn't perfect or doing a presentation that doesn't go fantastically doesn't mean you're not good enough.

You say sorry for asking a stupid question because you worry that you're not as clever as others in the room. But asking a question doesn't mean you're not smart enough.

You stay quiet in a meeting because your emotional brain doesn't want you to be kicked out of the pack. But it is not actually a life-or-death situation.

FIGHT, FLIGHT AND FREEZE

I recently received a great insight that could help you live a much less stressful life. It builds on the fight, flight and freeze responses.

People often point out that I don't get stressed very often. And it's true. My friends might say it is because I'm a very positive person or that it's in my nature to stay calm. However, after reading *The Chimp Paradox* I believe I don't get stressed because I'm happy making decisions.

The book talks about the natural instinct we all have when faced with an uncomfortable situation or decision: we either *fight, flight* or *freeze*.

If asked to do something out of their comfort zone like standing on stage, running a project or applying for a new role, many people will say, "No," which is the *flight* instinct. We don't want to do something so we effectively run away from it by saying no.

Perhaps you disagree with what someone is saying. They say something that triggers you and your emotional brain has the instinct to *fight*, which results in you telling them what you think of them. You feel outraged and you have an argument.

When you are put on the spot and asked a question, you may completely forget what you want to say. This is the *freeze* instinct and it is often the reaction people are most worried about with public speaking.

All three of these reactions are perfectly normal when your emotional brain is triggered by what it thinks is a difficult situation.

INDECISION

The newer concept for me was learning that when you experience fight, flight or freeze, you are deciding to do one of them. However, when you don't carry out one of these motions, you are not making a decision at all. You are in a state of indecision. Indecision causes adrenaline to be produced, which, coupled with a difficult situation, leads to anxiety and results in you feeling stressed.

In which situations do you feel stressed? Consider the decisions you could make to reduce your level of indecision and therefore lower your stress levels too.

If it is a decision to apply for a new job, making a decision is far less stressful than spending weeks thinking about it. Saying yes or no to an opportunity your boss thinks you should take is better than avoiding the conversation with them and hoping they don't ask you again. Deciding to ask a question in a meeting is less stressful than waiting to see if the perfect opportunity arises.

What decisions can you start making? The more decisions you make, the lower your anxiety levels will be and therefore the less stressed you'll feel.

THE COMPUTER BRAIN

The third part of your brain, alongside the emotional brain and the rational brain, is the computer. If you think of a literal computer, it may do things which seem automatic, but it actually happens because you tell it what to do. You need to type or click something or program the computer to make it do something.

Your computer brain isn't too different. It is trained by past experiences, memories and beliefs. It works automatically depending on what you've programmed it to do. It doesn't question anything. It looks at the database of beliefs and memories to determine what it will do.

Maybe your computer brain is programmed to say, "Sorry to ask a stupid question," every time you ask a question because your emotional brain remembers feeling stupid once when you asked a question at school. To protect itself, it programmed the computer brain to apologise when asking questions in case others judge you.

The good news is that you can reprogram your computer brain, just as you can reprogram a physical computer.

WHY DOESN'T OUR RATIONAL BRAIN TALK MORE?

Our rational brain often takes a backseat because the human brain hasn't evolved as fast as our lifestyles. For most of human history, survival was key and we had to rely on our emotional brain. Even though modern life is safer, the brain still defaults to survival mode when it senses a potential threat. It prioritises the emotional brain, cutting off signals from the rational brain and stopping our rational thinking. We find ourselves in fight, flight or freeze mode when it is unnecessary – we're overanalysing emails not speaking up in meetings and needlessly apologising.

This book is helping you to reprogram your brain.

SUMMARISING THE SCIENCE

If I were to summarise in one sentence how your brain works, what drives it and the impact it can have, it would be this:

Your brain is keeping you safe!

That is it. Quite simply. Your brain has one job. Your inner critic is trying to keep you safe.

Remind yourself from the previous chapter what your inner critic is saying and what story you are telling yourself. What is it stopping you from doing?

Now that you know your brain has just one job, to keep you safe, think about what your inner critic is trying to keep you safe *from*. Is it a fear of failing? Or a fear of success? Is it trying to keep you safe from being judged? From being different? Are you worried you're not good enough? Do you think you need to be perfect? Is it fear of abandonment or rejection?

— What is your inner critic trying to keep you safe from?

STAY SAFE AND DON'T APPLY FOR THAT JOB

Ever thought about applying for another job but then thought better of it and decided not to? Your inner critic was probably doing its thing and trying to keep you safe as one of my clients found.

We discovered that if she applied for a job, she would have to walk into the interview owning her successes. What if people thought she was arrogant? In her mind, arrogant people weren't nice. It went a step further for her than this. She had a belief that she had to be nice in order to be liked, otherwise she'd be rejected. She remembered how it felt as a child to be rejected. Her emotional brain was protecting her and therefore she didn't apply for the job. Phew!

When you see it laid out like this, you can spot the steps her brain took. But when your own brain does something similar, until you reflect or say it out loud, all that you see is that a job came up, you thought of applying and decided not to. The rational brain was not even engaged. You were not conscious of this decision-making process.

One of my clients recently told me, "It's good to get all this out and realise what I'm thinking so I can see it, describe it, assess it and challenge it," which is so true. It is hard to challenge it without going through those other steps first.

— **What is your inner critic trying to keep you safe from?**

THE WORST-CASE SCENARIO

There's a great book called *WFH (Working From Home): How To Build a Career You Love When You're Not in the Office* by Harriet Minter. About halfway through she asks, "What's the worst-case scenario for your career in five years' time?"

That question floored me. It took two days for me to process and fully answer it.

I was already a Senior Director, and my path was to become a Vice President within the next five years, maybe even two years. I was actively working towards it. Surprisingly, my first thought was, the worst-case scenario for my career in five years' time was becoming a Vice President still writing slide decks!

Then I thought, *No!* That was not the worst case. The worst case would be to try coaching and fail. What if I did what everyone told me I should do and started my own coaching business… and it failed? What if I let everyone down?

Again, I thought, *No!* That's not the worst case either. The worst case would be to have never tried coaching because I was too scared of failing.

I knew right then that I had to take action. I knew deep down I wanted to do this. I couldn't not do it just because I was scared of failing. I messaged my coach, Donna, who I'd been friends with for a couple of years, and said, "I'm in!" I was ready to be coached by her to help me take the steps I needed to believe in myself.

In my version of events that was it. I kicked fear out of the way, signed up for her coaching program, and fear never featured again. That version, of course, is not true! Donna reminded me a couple of years later that although I did message her saying I was in, I then asked about a thousand questions, and they were all coming from a place of fear. I know it has become a cliché, but I felt the fear and did it anyway and it was absolutely liberating.

"FEEL THE FEAR AND DO IT ANYWAY."

- Susan Jeffers

When I started being coached, my goal was to write a business plan so that one day, in five to ten years, if I wanted to leave my corporate job, I would have a plan.

In reality, I started my own business within three months of joining the program and had my first paying client. Within three more months, I set the date to leave my corporate job. I realised that my purpose in life was to positively impact the world.

Fast forward a couple of years, I have a successful international business coaching busy professionals, business owners and leaders. I deliver workshops for companies both big and small and I run coaching retreats. I love it, but more importantly, I am no longer driven by fear and I know I am positively impacting the world.

How about you in five years? What is your worst case?

To help you think, there's a worksheet for you called Your Perfect Life on the book resources page: https://www.tararulecoaching.com/book-downloads

What is the worst-case scenario for your career in five years' time? Is it to still be doing the same thing at the same company? Is it to have never followed your passion and purpose? Is it to feel stuck? To be doing a job you hate?

— What's the worst-case scenario for your career in five years' time?

"WHAT IF I FALL? OH BUT MY DARLING, WHAT IF YOU FLY?"

- Erin Hanson

What about the best case? Is it to be a Vice President at your company? To be a CEO? To be a leader? To be doing a job you love? To be running your own business? To feel happy and successful?

— What is the best-case scenario for your career in five years' time?

Reflect again and dig even deeper into what your inner critic is trying to keep you safe from.

— What is your inner critic trying to keep you safe from?

You may have taken a while to answer these questions about your worst-case scenario for your career. If you have written something down, great. If you have paused and reflected, that's amazing too. If you have skimmed these questions, take a moment longer to reflect. The more you know who you are, what triggers you and what you really want, the happier and more successful you can be. Feel free to return to this later if you find it hard.

BUT WHAT IF I FAIL?

I had a big fear of failing. Nowadays, I am in control of that fear most of the time. Every so often it still pops up, but I am so much better able to control it. You can control your fear too.

As I have already said, my fear of failing is driven by how I felt when I didn't pass my exams when I was twelve. We have looked at how the brain works, and now you're invited to go even deeper and reflect on why *your* fear is there.

One of my clients was working full-time in a corporate job, and his dream was to start his own business. He said he knew he needed to start posting on social media, which he wasn't doing!

We started to dig into what was stopping him and unearthed that he had made up a story. He believed that when he posted on social media about his business, he would lose all his privacy. His fear came from not wanting to be vulnerable, and believing he had to keep everything private in order to be safe.

All of this was being driven by his emotional brain, without him knowing why.

His thought was that he wanted to post on social media. But his *action* was to decide not to. When we started to unpick it, he realised that a whole lot of fear was driving the action, or in this case, inaction.

He had grown up being told from a very young age to keep what went on at home a secret: to keep quiet, to keep what happened behind closed doors, not to open up to other people and *never* to be vulnerable. His brain was trying to keep him safe. It was keeping his six-year-old self safe!

Once he became aware of this it all clicked into place. He didn't want to post on social media about his business because of his fear of other people knowing what was going on and that feeling of being vulnerable.

By naming his fear he brought it from his subconscious into his conscious. Once it was out in the open and in his conscious brain he could start to challenge it with his rational brain. Now he was aware of his deep-rooted fear, many options and actions became possible.

It was amazing to be a part of his realisation.

BUT WHAT IF I AM SUCCESSFUL?

You may be surprised to hear that many people are scared of being successful. I have worked with people who are scared of being successful because they think their family will judge them. Perhaps they will no longer fit in with their friends. If they believe that they *could* be successful, they've got no excuses to not try and that in itself can feel scary.

Maybe you worry about the 'what ifs' of success too? What if everything changes? Often, we hate change because we find it scary. Change can bring a lot of emotion and uncertainty which our brains don't like.

Your brain is trying to keep you safe, so if you stay where you are, doing what you've always done, it feels safe and you don't need to worry about all the 'what ifs'.

Which is stronger for you? A fear of failing or a fear of success? Or is it a mix of both?

WHAT DOES YOUR FEAR LOOK LIKE?

Let's take a look at your fear and start to recognise yours.

- **The biggest fear that holds me back is…** (Fear of failing, success, looking stupid, being vulnerable, etc.)

- **When do you first remember having this feeling?** (Is there a childhood memory or more recent memory when you felt like this?)

- **Where do you think this fear came from?** (Failing an exam, feedback you were given, feeling alone, etc.)

- **What is this fear, this feeling, your inner critic *really* trying to keep you safe from?** (Allow yourself to dig deep.)

It is ok if you feel like this has opened up something for you. You are not alone. If you find it difficult to reflect on these fears and feel triggered in any way, you can reach out to me by contacting me: my details are at the end of this book. But also, reach out to a friend. Tell someone close to you how you feel.

It is likely that something happened in your past to impact your confidence which results in you now apologising. We can't change the past, but when we understand where something came from it is so much easier to choose something different.

When people tune into their subconscious and start naming their fears out loud, they often say "this sounds crazy" or "I know this may sound weird but..." Only when you give your inner critic a voice and listen to it, do you realise that it isn't telling the truth at all and you can start to challenge it. You realise that it sounds crazy or weird. However, while it remains in your subconscious, your brain takes it as fact. You silence your inner critic by listening to it first.

Before we look at the choices that now open up for you, let's take a moment to celebrate. Celebrate you! Firstly, for doing this work to understand yourself more, but also, let's celebrate this voice in your head!

THANK YOU

You may have uncovered your inner critic's fear of failing, of not being good enough, not being enough. It may be scared of looking stupid, being judged, or being abandoned. Perhaps it is worried people won't take you seriously or you'll stand out. Your inner critic may be scared of success.

It is amazing that you have a voice in your head so protective of you that it will do anything to keep you safe. Imagine having a best friend who was that protective of you. There is only one thing you could say to them: thank you.

I thank Dobby for trying to keep me safe, for trying to protect me so I don't fail, so I never feel how that twelve-year-old girl felt ever again, like she wasn't good enough. Say thank you to your inner critic! Say it out loud, write it down, or think it in your head, but whatever you do, say thank you. Embrace it and love it.

It is not about telling that inner critic to shut up and put it in a box, because that won't work. Your subconscious is very powerful. Its only job is to keep you safe, so trying to forget your fears, putting them in a box and getting on with things isn't effective. But when you embrace them and say thank you, you get to move forward and choose something different.

Let's say thank you.

— **"Thank You." (Say it out loud or write it down here.)**

SUMMARY - YOU HAD ONE JOB

- When you apologise all the time, the impact can be huge. You are not taken seriously, are seen as weak, and are less likely to be able to influence and get what you want.
- Your emotional brain is in charge of your actions and reactions. It senses fear and its job is to keep you safe.
- The emotional brain hasn't evolved to keep pace with the world we live in. It is still in survival mode.
- Your subconscious looks to your past experiences to drive automatic behaviour.
- Your brain is trying to keep you safe even when there isn't a real and present threat.
- This can lead to procrastination and too much apologising.
- Fight, Flight or Freeze are normal reactions when your emotional brain is triggered by a difficult situation.
- Indecision leads to stress. Therefore, it is healthier to make decisions than to stay in indecision.
- Your computer brain is 'automatic' but can be reprogrammed.
- In summary, your brain and your inner critic are trying to keep you safe.
- When you think about the worst-case scenario for your career in five years' time, your inner critic is trying to keep you safe from something.
- Imagine the best case!
- When you name your fear, you bring your subconscious thoughts into your consciousness so your rational brain can then challenge it.

- Say, "Thank you," to your inner critic. It is amazing that you have a part of your brain trying so hard to keep you safe.

REFLECT

Take a moment to pause and write down your answers to these three questions.

— **What is the worst-case scenario for your career in five years' time?**

— **What is your inner critic stopping you from doing?**

— **What is your inner critic trying to keep you safe from?**

What else do you want to remember from this chapter?

5
CHOOSE YOUR INNER CHEERLEADER

Once you are fully aware of what your inner critic is telling you and why, you have a choice. You get to choose continuing to listen to your inner critic or starting to listen to your inner cheerleader. You get to choose if you carry on being driven by fear or something different. This chapter is all about helping you discover what that something different is.

IF YOU STAY COMFORTABLE

It feels safe to listen to your inner critic. It may not feel great, but it feels safe. If you never put yourself out there, you'll never fail. If you never apply for another job, you'll never be rejected. If you never talk assertively, you'll never be told no.

But *is* it safe? If you never put yourself out there, you'll never know what's possible. If you never apply for another job, you'll never know if it was your dream job. If you never talk assertively, you'll never get what you really want.

CHOOSE YOUR INNER CHEERLEADER

What will *you* never know, never achieve, never feel if you play it safe and listen to your inner critic forever?

That fear of failure could have stopped me asking for a pay rise when I was eighteen, starting a new job in which I felt I had no idea what I was doing, going for a promotion two grades above me, leaving my corporate job and starting my own business, posting videos on social media... writing this book. It could have stopped me doing so many things.

It would have stopped me getting a bigger pay rise when I was eighteen, joining a company I loved working at, letting my boss know I was serious about my career, being the CEO and Founder of my own business, being a positive force online (people often tell me I'm the most positive person they know on social media), and it would have stopped me from having a positive impact on you with this book.

But I got to choose and so do you.

— **What could your inner critic stop you from doing?**

— **What could be possible if you felt the fear and did it anyway?**

INTRODUCING YOUR INNER CHEERLEADER

It is time we properly met and got to know your inner cheerleader. Your inner cheerleader is that voice inside you that says, "You can do it," and, "You've got this," and, "You are good enough." It is often a little voice. Your inner cheerleader can be quiet. They may not speak up very often. You may ignore them most of the time. But they are there, just like your inner critic.

What is your inner cheerleader trying to say to you? Mine says that I am good enough, I am a successful entrepreneur, I am a good mum, I can do this, and I can help people.

People I work with have said that their inner cheerleaders are telling them they have lots of experience, their opinion is important, they are great at their job and they can do it. One person's says, "You are enough and you have everything you need to succeed." Another's says, "You are good enough, you haven't just been lucky. You deserve this."

It is time to tune into *your* inner cheerleader. Take a deep breath, smile and listen.

— **What is your inner cheerleader trying to say to you?**

How did it feel to tune in for a moment and listen? If you skimmed over this question, allow yourself to take a deep breath, smile and say in your head, "What do you want to tell me, cheerleader?" and see what comes up for you.

THE TRUTH

Let's rephrase the same topic in a slightly different way. If you don't resonate so much with the term 'inner cheerleader', answer instead the question, "What is your truth?" I often ask my clients this question. The things our inner critic tells us often are not true! It is not true that you're not good enough; it is not true that you don't deserve to be happy and successful; it is not true that you have to be perfect.

So instead:

- **What is your truth?**

Some people find this step of listening to their inner cheerleader quite easy, but others resist it. Wherever you are in this process, it is ok. You are ok. You are exactly where you're meant to be. I invite you again to be kind to yourself. Allow yourself to listen to those kind words from your inner cheerleader. Take the time you need and come back to these questions later if you need to.

What are you hearing and feeling? Write it down, even if you don't believe it *yet*.

'Yet' is such a powerful word. It gives you hope because it may not be instant, but if you give it time, if you make a conscious decision to listen to your inner cheerleader and if you practise listening to them every day, you will start to believe them.

- **What else does your inner cheerleader want to tell you?**

GET CLOSER TO YOUR INNER CHEERLEADER

Just as we did with your inner critic, let's get to know your inner cheerleader a bit more. What does your inner cheerleader look, sound or feel like?

My inner cheerleader is a warm, comforting feeling around my heart. I breathe in when I listen to her and I feel my chest and heart expand. She's a she, even though I have no image of her at all.

Clients have described their inner cheerleaders in various ways. One pictures a big, smiling character full of energy, with a big laugh, and wearing lots of makeup and bright clothes. Another says their cheerleader wears a sequin dress and they can hear the shimmer of the sequins when they walk. Another hears the rustle of the pompoms as their inner cheerleader picks them up. One says their inner cheerleader looks like them.

How about you? Take some time to draw them below, write bullet points, do a mind map, or whatever feels good to you. How does it feel to listen to your inner cheerleader? Does it feel weird? Emotional? Are they used to being listened to?

— **What does your inner cheerleader look, feel or sound like?**

CHOOSE YOUR INNER CHEERLEADER

There is a great book called *The Big Leap* by Gay Hendricks. He invites you to say a mantra: "I expand in abundance, success, and love every day, as I inspire those around me to do the same." I have adapted it slightly so it rolls off my tongue. Mine is: "I expand with success, love and abundance and I inspire others to do the same." When I make the conscious decision to listen to my inner cheerleader, I often start by breathing in, expanding my chest, smiling and saying this mantra in my mind. Then I ask my inner cheerleader what she wants to remind me of right now.

Try it for yourself.

TIME FOR SOMETHING NEW

What is important, is that you get to choose.

You get to choose every day whether you listen to your inner cheerleader or your inner critic.
You get to choose whether you make decisions based on fear or possibility.
You get to choose whether you say sorry at the start of every sentence or if you sound more assertive.

"WHAT GOT YOU HERE WON'T GET YOU THERE."

- Marshall Goldsmith

It is time to choose something different. It is time to embrace a new belief.

Those things your inner critic tells you are often called limiting beliefs. When you say things that sound like fact, such as, "I can't", "I'm not" or, "I'll never" they are beliefs that limit your potential. But the thing with beliefs is that they are *not* facts: they are just things you've told yourself thousands of times. You get to choose to rewire your brain with a new belief.

What do you choose to believe instead?

Let's take those limiting beliefs one by one. Write down what your inner critic has been telling you. Then challenge them one by one. Ask yourself each time, "Is it true?" Then ask yourself what your inner cheerleader wants to tell you instead.

I have been coached and have worked on my own development over many years. When I became aware of my limiting beliefs I wrote them down. I then drew a line through them and wrote down what I chose to believe instead. Here are some of mine. You will see how many and how varied they are. Perhaps some will resonate with you.

Old Belief: What my inner critic told me	New Belief: What my inner cheerleader wanted to tell me
I'm not good enough.	I am enough.
I'm not an entrepreneur.	I am a successful entrepreneur. (At first, I have lots of entrepreneurial qualities.)
I'm not a good mum.	I'm a great, loving mum.
I have no USP (Unique Selling Point).	My USP is being me!
Dieting is hard!	I love my body and I'm excited to take care of it and feel fitter and healthier.
I can't find anyone to deliver a workshop on Stop Apologising.	I will create, deliver and write Stop Apologising.
Selling my coaching is awkward.	Selling my coaching means I will help people.

Your turn!

What are some of your beliefs that you are now aware your inner critic is telling you?

1. Write them in the first column.

2. Ask yourself, one by one, "Is it true?"

3. In the second column write what your inner cheerleader wants to tell you so you can start choosing those new beliefs.

Old Belief: What your inner critic is telling you	New Belief: What your inner cheerleader wants to tell you

How does it feel to challenge those old beliefs? How does it feel to listen to your inner cheerleader?

Does it feel good? Do you feel lighter? Are you smiling?

Or… do you feel good for an instant but then challenge whether your inner cheerleader is telling you the truth? If so, that is just your inner critic trying to keep you safe. It is scared of what might happen or what you might do if you listen to your inner cheerleader more, if you believe in yourself, if you grow in confidence. It doesn't know what will happen then and that can feel scary. Your inner critic would rather be stagnant and safe than go for it into the unknown.

If this is you, remind yourself that you *are* safe and listen to your inner cheerleader even more.

WHO DO YOU THINK YOU ARE?

The more you choose to listen to your inner cheerleader, the easier it will get. However, that inner critic can be strong. It takes continual work to consciously choose to listen to your inner cheerleader.

Here is a real and current example. Although I have done so much work on my own beliefs and I now listen to my inner cheerleader much more than my inner critic, while I write this book my inner critic has been jumping up and down, saying, "Hang on! Who are you to write a book? You've not done all your own research, you're not a professor, you didn't even go to university!"

Breaking it down, I know that Dobby, my inner critic is scared. He is afraid of no one buying the book. He is afraid of me saying something that people disagree with. He is afraid that no one will like it. This is driven by fear: fear of not being liked, fear of failing, fear that it won't be good enough… fear that *I* won't be good enough!

I know that Dobby is trying to keep me safe. I am quickly able to spot this voice and this fear. I have asked, is it true that if no one reads my book it means I'm not good enough and a failure? No! I choose to listen to my inner cheerleader who is telling me that I can positively impact you and thousands of others by writing this down, that I am great at simplifying the complex so I can explain all the 'sciency' bits, and that I have helped many people feel more confident so I know what I'm talking about.

I have reminded myself that I get to choose, and I choose to write this book so I can help you and so many others and make a positive impact on the world.

LET'S GET BUILDING

The trick is to keep building.

If you wanted to build a wall, you wouldn't build the first row of bricks then stop and give up or kick it down because it didn't look like a wall. You know you need to build row after row on top of each other before a wall appears. It is small to start with but before you know it, it is huge.

The same is true for your confidence.

You may have built the first layer just now by listening to your inner cheerleader. So well done. The foundations are there and you've started. But tomorrow something may knock your confidence. Do you choose to knock that first layer of bricks down and beat yourself up that you're not confident yet, or do you choose to say that it is ok, you just have more work to do? Listen to that inner cheerleader again and build the next layer.

Hopefully, you don't give up. To build your confidence, build layer on layer. Listen to your inner cheerleader over and over again. Stretch out of your comfort zone over and over again and see that you are ok and you are growing. Practise, get feedback and never give up.

You can keep building by using Part Two of this book. It is crammed full of practical tools that you can put into practice to help you stop apologising and feel more confident. Before you reach Part Two, you can build on your layers by becoming more aware of your emotions and choosing more positive emotions.

POSITIVITY BOOST

Research shows that you need to experience three positive emotions for every negative emotion you have in order to flourish, feel good, function well and thrive. It is not about cutting out all negative emotions but experiencing enough positive emotions so you can bounce back quickly.

You can boost those emotions in many ways. You could think about what you're grateful for, look out the window and be in awe of nature, close your eyes and take a deep breath for some serenity, phone a friend for some laughter, look at photos of some fun memories, remember a funny story, watch a funny video, or one of my favourites, put on a song that makes you feel good.

You can boost those emotions reactively when you notice you're feeling down and do something to counter it. Or you can boost those emotions proactively so that when something happens to pull you down, you bounce back quickly.

In fact, give yourself three minutes right now to listen to a song that you love and makes you feel good. Dance around the kitchen, sing out loud, sit on the sofa and shimmy, shut your eyes on the train and smile. Whatever is right for you.

I invite you to give yourself a little burst of positive energy right now before you do the next bit of reflection. If you want to borrow one of my uplifting songs then I highly recommend *Proud Mary* by Tina Turner, *Wake Me Up Before You Go-Go* by Wham! or *Fight Song* by Rachel Platten.

Take a pic of you reading this book and tag me on social media with your song because I am always looking to expand my list of feel-good songs. (You can find out how to contact me at the end of this book.)

Go do it!

EXCUSES, EXCUSES

It is often easy to spot when you're listening to your inner critic, because it gives you so many excuses.

For example, you do a great presentation and you say "Yes, but the audience were kind to me and didn't ask me any difficult questions" or you get offered a new job and you say "Yes, but that's because I'm good building relationships" or you hit your goals and you say "Yes, but I had a lot of support along the way"

The fabulous book *The Secret Thoughts of Successful Women* by Valerie Young contains brilliant exercises which inspired this exercise.

First, you write down everything you've accomplished in your life, goals you've hit, things you feel proud of. You take time to look at the evidence, the facts, with no excuses. Stick with the what, when and where.

For example:

- Passing your driving test.
- Getting a job.
- Qualifications.
- Bonuses.
- Good feedback you've had about presentations you've delivered, projects you've run or things you've created.
- Targets you've hit.
- Sales you've made.
- Objectives you've hit.
- Promotions you've received.

CHOOSE YOUR INNER CHEERLEADER

Write them now in the first column of the table below. Titled 'Your accomplishments through life'.

Once you've written them all down, allow your inner critic some airspace. Remember, you don't need to put your inner critic in a box and pretend they're not there. It is much better to listen to your inner critic so you can start to challenge them.

Write down all the excuses your inner critic is giving. Like:

- It only happened because people like me.
- I was lucky.
- I knew someone who offered me the job.
- It was just good timing.

Write down all those excuses in the second column. Titled 'Excuses from your inner critic'.

Now thank your inner critic for trying to keep you safe. Next, fill in the third column with what is actually true. Titled 'What is really true? Listen to your inner cheerleader'.

What does your inner cheerleader want to remind you? Perhaps:

- I am good at what I do.
- I worked hard for this.
- I have a lot of experience.

Even if there was a bit of luck, or you knew someone, or the timing was right, you are the one who made it happen. Outside factors may have helped but they don't take away from you or your achievements.

Your accomplishments through life	Excuses from your inner critic	What is really true? Listen to your inner cheerleader

How does it feel to identify the excuses your inner critic comes up with to keep you safe? Remembering your inner cheerleader knows what's really true.

If you skimmed over the earlier questions about what your inner cheerleader wants to say to you, now is the time to dig deep, smile and listen to them.

- **What does your inner cheerleader want to remind you of, based on this chapter?**

"YOU GET TO CHOOSE WHO YOU LISTEN TO."

- Tara Rule

It is true that you get to choose. However, only *you* can make that decision. I can't make you listen to your inner cheerleader, your partner can't make you believe you are good enough, and your boss can't make you believe in yourself. However, you *can!* You get to choose. So, are you ready?

— **Do you choose to listen to your inner cheerleader more?**

TIME TO OWN IT!

When you have been listening to your inner cheerleader, you've probably so far written down statements like, you are good enough, you can do this, you do deserve to be happy and successful, all in third person.

They are all fabulous, but let's now turn them into I AM statements. Let's get it to a point where you really own it. You are good enough *becomes* I am good enough. You can do this *becomes* I am doing this. You deserve to be happy and successful *becomes* I am happy and successful.

This is important because the switch makes it easier for your brain to believe. When you put statements in the present tense and the first person, you build more hope that you can achieve it. You are programming your computer brain, feeding it new beliefs which are more helpful than the old beliefs which are driven by fear.

— **What are your I AM statements?**

It doesn't stop there, though.

- Write them down on separate pieces of paper where you can see them and read them often.
- Write them on post-it notes and stick them to your bathroom mirror, your laptop, your bedside table.
- Say these statements before you go to bed and when you wake up.

You need to train your brain to *believe* these new beliefs. The best way to do that is to tell yourself them over and over again. Let's start to counter the hundreds of times your inner critic has told you the opposite.

— **How can you remind yourself of your I AM statements?**

Imagine waking up every morning and reminding yourself just how amazing you are and what is possible. Imagine being driven by possibility and taking action based on possibility, hope and positivity instead of taking action (or inaction) driven by fear.

SUMMARY - YOU GET TO CHOOSE

- You get to choose if you carry on being driven by fear, or if you instead choose something different.
- By listening to your inner critic and staying safe, you could miss out on many great opportunities.
- What is your inner cheerleader trying to tell you?
- By challenging your inner critic, you can start to tune into your truth instead.
- Allow yourself to picture your inner cheerleader. What do they look, sound and feel like?
- It can take time and practice to listen to your inner cheerleader and that is ok.
- Repeat after me: 'I expand with success, love and abundance and I inspire others to do the same.'
- By looking at your beliefs one by one, you can challenge them and create new beliefs.
- Beliefs are just things you have told yourself thousands of times. They are not facts.
- Like building a wall, building your confidence takes time. Focus on one brick at a time.
- You need three positive emotions for every negative emotion in order to flourish in life.
- Find an uplifting song and hit play to boost your positive emotions instantly.
- Challenge the excuses your inner critic is feeding you.
- Create your I AM statements so that your brain starts believing new beliefs.

REFLECT

Take a moment to pause and write down your answers to these three questions.

— **What could be possible if you felt the fear and did it anyway?**

— **What does your inner cheerleader want to remind you?**

— **What do you choose?**

What else do you want to remember from this chapter?

YOUR MINDSET RULES

A massive well done for working through Part One.

Before we move into Part Two, which is full of tools to stop apologising and feel more confident, take a moment to reflect on all that you've just unpacked and look at Your Mindset Rules.

You can download a PDF of Your Mindset Rules here: https://www.tararulecoaching.com/book-downloads

Your Mindset Rules were created to help you understand what you tell yourself and why. This gives you the power to choose something different so you are powered by belief and positivity instead of driven by fear.

Your Mindset Rules are:

Reflect on your story.
Understand the impact.
Love that it is keeping you safe.
Embrace a new belief.
Strengthen with commitment.

We have touched on all of these through Part One so take a moment to write down your reflections for each of the following questions.

Reflect on your story. What is your inner critic telling you? Listen to that voice in your head: what does it believe? What is it telling you that could be holding you back? Remember to be kind to yourself as everyone has an inner critic.

— **What is your inner critic telling you?**

Understand the impact. What is it stopping you from doing? When you are driven by fear, when you listen to that inner critic of yours, there are so many things you could do but don't, just in case your inner critic is right!

— **What is it stopping you from doing?**

Love that your inner critic is keeping you safe. What is it keeping you safe from? Remember that your emotional brain has one job and that is to keep you safe. It is not driven by rational thoughts, but it thinks it is protecting you.

— **What is your inner critic keeping you safe from?**

Embrace a new belief. What do you choose to believe instead? The good news is that you also have an inner cheerleader, and the even better news is that you get to choose to listen to them instead. You get to choose something different.

— **What do you choose to believe instead?**

Strengthen with commitment. What is your 'I AM statement'? When you turn what your inner cheerleader says to you into an I AM statement, you feed a more positive belief into your subconscious so you start taking action because of possibility instead of fear.

— **What is your 'I AM statement'?**

These are Your Mindset Rules. Mark this page, write them down in your notes if you're listening to this book or fill in the worksheet online. Have them so you can access them easily whenever you need to get your mindset in a place that will help instead of hinder you.

CONGRATULATIONS

By reading this book, you are one step closer to choosing something different and believing in yourself. Let's celebrate that.

Part One has explained the what and the why of apologising and you have reflected on what drives you. Step into Part Two for the tools, frameworks and examples to help you further.

To feel more confident as soon as you finish this book, start putting into practice what you've learnt so far *now*. Imagine what your life could look like in one year if you stop apologising. You could silence your inner critic, find your confidence and stop saying sorry!

PART TWO

AWARENESS IS GREAT BUT NOT ENOUGH

You know that you apologise too much: that is why you picked up this book. Either the title spoke to you or a friend bought it for you (in which case, you have a fabulous friend). You want to stop apologising and feel more confident, but you find it hard. You want to do something different but can't (yet). Want to know why?

It is because awareness isn't enough.

Awareness is often the first step, but it is not the only step. *Knowing* about the problem doesn't *solve* it.

Just because you *know* there is a problem, doesn't mean you take the steps to change. How often have you been aware that you *should* end a relationship, eat healthier or have a difficult conversation? But you don't do it. You put it off, maybe for a few hours, days or years. Maybe you never do it, even though you are aware of what needs to happen.

Years ago, when I was the chair of the Women's Network at O2, I went to a diversity and inclusion event. The theme of the event was unconscious bias and how to help people become more aware of it, to create change.

One of the speakers shared a great story and model.

"I used to be overweight," he said. "I was *aware* that I was overweight. I was *aware* of the reasons why I should lose weight. And I was *aware* how I could lose weight. But I didn't!"

Sound familiar? Awareness is good, but it's not the answer.

The speaker shared that once you are aware of something, these simple elements (beyond awareness) make the difference:

1. Motivation - Knowing your why.

2. Simple rules - Understanding how, by having a list of rules you can stick to.
3. Tools - Having support in place so you can be successful.

He brought it to life for us by putting it into the context of losing weight. I will share it with you before we look at it through a *stop apologising* lens.

1. Motivation

Figure out your motivation for losing weight. This is personal to you. Allow yourself to go deep. What personal benefit could you see? Could you improve your overall well-being? Could you live a long, healthy and happy life? Could you set a good example for your kids?

2. Simple rules

Next, think of some simple rules that will make a difference. This could include drinking two litres of water every day, doing a workout four days a week or eating five fruit and veg a day.

3. Tools

Finally, use helpful tools like a calorie counting app and a smartwatch or have support by joining a gym.

Having thought about these three elements, it will be so much easier to lose weight. You are much more likely to hit your goals than if you just have awareness.

Let's bring this to life within the context of apologising.

1. Motivation

Why do you want to stop apologising? What could happen for you if you sounded more assertive? Is it so people take you more seriously, to get that promotion or so you feel more confident? Get specific. What's your why?

2. Simple Rules

What rules could you put in place? You could re-read emails to check your language, begin every morning listening to your inner cheerleader or replace the word *sorry* with *thank you*. (Don't worry if you don't know yet. This part of the book will offer you lots of Rules to choose from.)

3. Tools

Use helpful tools like the frameworks in this chapter or get support and accountability through a friend or coach.

While this model is simple, it takes thought. The Rules and Tools in this chapter will help.

Take a moment to note down any thoughts that have already come to you.

— Motivation - What is your why? Why do you want to stop apologising?

— Simple Rules - What rules could you put in place? What do you already know you could do more of or differently?

— **Tools - What tools can support you? Who can support you?**

As you read this part, don't forget to mark or write down the stories and tools that are most helpful to you. Circle the elements you love or pause the audiobook so you can make a note of what you would love to apply.

ONCE UPON A TIME

Introducing you to your cast of characters.

You will hear the tools and frameworks in Part Two brought to life as stories. These stories draw from coaching sessions, conversations with colleagues and friends and my own examples.

To respect everyone's anonymity and confidentiality, I have accumulated the examples and brought them to you through a cast of fictitious characters. They are amalgamations of real people so you will probably spot elements of yourself in them.

Let's meet them:

Maria is ambitious, enthusiastic, very talkative and appears confident. However, inside she has no idea what everyone else sees in her. She would love to start managing people soon, but at the same time does not know if she is ready to take that leap. Her favourite line is, "Sorry, this might be a stupid question."

Neesha is a mum first and career woman second. She manages a small team and is not sure how to be a great mum and a great manager at the same time. She feels overwhelmed when senior people are in the room and she wishes she had more hours in the day. Her favourite line is, "Sorry to take up your time."

Daniel is ambitious and smart. He works hard and progressed quickly after graduating from university. He was once told, "Don't be too personal at work," and, "Keep your private life separate." He realises he has been telling himself an unhelpful story and has worked hard to get in tune with what holds him back. He would love to have his own business and his favourite line is, "I know I'm overthinking this."

Lucy is a competitive teenager. She is empathetic and kind but doesn't love to talk about her feelings. Her mum grew up apologising too much and is trying to teach her daughter the importance of self-talk. Lucy's favourite line is, "I could have done better."

Anastasia has a good job in a good company, but years ago she had feedback that impacts how she shows up now, twenty years later. She grew up in a different country from where she now lives and feels that people read her wrong because what comes naturally to her isn't the accepted culture. Her favourite line is, "Sorry to interrupt."

Jada is a senior leader who has done very well throughout her career, but feels like she is juggling everything and isn't sure when it will all come crashing down. People come to her for advice all the time so she supposes they must see something in her but most days she is not quite sure what. Her favourite line is, "I'm just lucky."

Which character resonates most with you? Can you see yourself in one or all of them?

STOP
APOLOGISING
STORIES

SORRY FOR NOT REPLYING SOONER

Neesha loves to apologise. Sometimes it is appropriate for her to apologise, but often it is not.

Let's start with when it is ok for her to apologise. When her son has a tantrum because he doesn't want to put his shoes on for school this creates a ripple effect. They get stuck in traffic, arrive at school late, Neesha has to go into reception to drop him off and then gets stuck in more traffic.

Unfortunately, Neesha's nine am meeting is the victim of this episode and she turns up fifteen minutes late. Should she apologise? Yes. Is it polite to apologise? Yes. And does she apologise? Yes. Does she need to go into a five-minute story of just how badly her day is going so far and how bad her son's tantrum was? *No.*

Talking to my daughter about this book, I explained how people often say sorry when they don't need to. Her response was, "So, if I accidentally kick you in the face does that mean I don't need to apologise to you?" I am not sure what she thinks she'd be doing to accidentally kick me in the face, but my response was, "Yes, when you do something by accident and you hurt someone you absolutely should say sorry, but people often apologise when they don't need to."

And Neesha definitely apologises when she doesn't need to.

When she replies to emails, she often starts by saying, "Sorry for not getting back to you sooner," even though she is replying in less than twenty-four hours.

Unless you work in a role with strict rules on how quickly you respond, you don't need to apologise for not getting back sooner. You could say, "Thanks for your patience," but is that needed if you're replying the same day or the next day?

Next time you go to apologise, step back and ask yourself, "Do I need to apologise?" If not, don't!

If you do need to, remember:

1. It is ok to apologise when it is the polite thing to do.
2. You don't need to keep saying sorry – once is fine.
3. You don't need to give the other person your life story.

TOOL:

Before apologising, start this new habit. Pause for a second and ask yourself, "Do I need to apologise right now?"

SORRY DINNER IS LATE

When you say sorry too much, especially starting a sentence with an apology, you plant a negative thought in someone's head.

As we know, Neesha loves apologising, especially when it's not needed.

A perfect example is when she cooks dinner. She works full time, has a young boy at school and although she and her husband share lots around the house and with their son, Neesha is the one who does most of the cooking.

She has the best laid plans most nights. Once their son is in bed, she starts cooking with the aim that she and her husband can sit down at eight pm and enjoy a nice meal together.

However, with kids (and life) things don't often go exactly as planned and the eight pm timeline she sets herself rarely gets hit. Dinner is ready at twenty past eight and what is the first thing she says to her husband?

"Sorry dinner is late."

They have no plans that evening and are not running late for anything. Eight was simply a time Neesha had planned in her head to eat.

Her husband now has a negative thought planted in his head, though. He is thinking that dinner is late and may be annoyed or disappointed. He says, "That's ok," but they have started dinner on a bit of a negative note.

This may not seem huge. But it is not needed.

Neesha could have said, "Dinner is ready," to which he would have simply said, "Thank you." A much better way to start a meal together.

Why does Neesha say sorry so much? She says it is simply a habit.

A habit is an action driven by your subconscious. You are often not consciously aware you're doing it. At some point in time, your brain was fed a belief that it needed to do something. You start doing it and before you know it your subconscious has taken over and made it an automatic action. In Neesha's case, it was that she needed to apologise when running late.

It happens to so many of us, so remember to be kind to yourself if you spot yourself apologising as a habit. Habits can be broken and new habits can be formed. Neesha became aware that she apologised unnecessarily and decided to start a new habit of purely saying, "Dinner's ready," each night she cooked.

She didn't change the habit the instant she became aware of it, but she did start trying to remove the word sorry. It took a while to get used to it, but she persisted and now dinner starts on a better note. A bigger impact than that is the pride she feels in herself that she kicked that habit. She knows she can kick even more habits.

EXERCISE:

When do you apologise out of habit? Spend a few minutes writing them down below and then write what phrases you could say instead. Start forming that new habit today.

— **Your habits and replacement phrases are...**

SORRY FOR CRYING

Ever apologised for showing emotion? Do you say sorry when you cry? Do you hold the tears back?

Jada is super successful. She is focussed on her career but also on her personal development. She invested in herself and went on an amazing mind, body and soul retreat in France.

She knows she won't be successful by setting big goals alone. She needs to know what really stops her from being the best possible version of herself. What makes it even better is that she is in a room full of people also looking to unlock their full potential.

The coaches running the retreat know they need to help Jada probe further, to unearth the beliefs deep inside herself that she formed as a child. She is in a room surrounded by love and support so when she is asked to share her reflections, she does. And she quickly starts crying.

"I'm sorry for crying," she says straight away.

She isn't the only one to cry on that retreat, and she isn't the only one to apologise for it. One after another, when the women share, they cry. Some cry within the first hour and some on the last day. But the thing so many of them have in common is that they apologise for crying.

Jada is working through deep emotions and unlocking all sorts from her subconscious, but her number one priority is to apologise to the others in the room for showing her emotions and crying.

Why?

When you're a child and you cry, the first thing you hear is often, "It's ok, there's no need to cry, stop crying," so you take a breath and stop crying like you've been told. At the same time, you start to form a belief that crying is bad and you should stop it as soon as possible.

When you think about this, what do you remember being told as a child when you cried?

Remember, crying is just showing emotion, and emotions are good. When we laugh and feel love we embrace those emotions. However, we are trained from a young age to suppress emotions that are not seen as positive.

Notice that I didn't say 'negative' emotions. Why? Because then you may think they are bad when they are not. They are just emotions and we all have them. It is ok to feel angry, upset, sad and frustrated. The thing to be aware of is that you are in control of your actions. You can feel angry or frustrated but it is up to you if you decide to then shout, scream or storm out of the room, or if you process those emotions in a more productive way. Suppressing them is not the answer.

We often learn to suppress emotions because we don't want other people to feel uncomfortable. When we see someone cry, we want to help them feel better but we don't always know how, so we tell them to stop. Before you know it, we are suppressing our emotions.

But the emotions don't disappear. They stay deep within you ready to come out when you do not expect it. It could be that your kids say something and you snap at them, you suddenly burst into tears at an advert on TV, or you get given some feedback at work and you feel like you've been punched in the stomach and argue back.

Those emotions are still there underneath that fake smile.

With Jada, when she apologised for crying during her retreat, her coach invited her to stop apologising. She reminded her that she was in a safe space, she was safe and it was ok to cry. A few minutes later, having let the emotion out rather than bottling it up, she felt lighter and a huge sense of relief.

Later that day when Jada felt the emotions come again, she caught her coach's eye and instead of apologising she let the emotions be. This allowed her to keep her focus on herself and process her emotions instead of worrying about the others in the room.

REMEMBER:

Next time you feel like crying, cry! Unapologetically.

When you are next with a friend or loved one who is crying, try to resist telling them to stop crying. Instead, hold space for them and show them love.

SORRY, BUT I'VE JUST GOT A QUESTION

Why do we do this? Ruin a perfectly good and assertive question with 'little words'! In this story title it is the word *just* (not to mention the *sorry*).

Other examples are: *probably* and *I think*. They are filler words that aren't meant literally. You may know something with total certainty, but you'll add the word *probably* as a filler. Maybe the filler words you overuse are *please* and *thank you*.

Sorry can become a filler word too. You say it but you don't mean it at all: "Sorry, but I'm going to bed now." You are not necessarily sorry, you are just tired and going to bed. "Sorry, can I sit here?" when you want to take a seat on the train. You are not sorry for wanting to sit down.

Don't get me wrong, I love manners. I was brought up with manners and I try to instil manners in my girls too. But are you being polite or are you saying please and thank you so much that it is meaningless? Even worse, does it weaken your message?

Neesha told me she apologises so much at home that the word sorry is now kind of meaningless. She knows it is a learnt behaviour. Her mum apologises a lot and now she does too. But her son hears her saying sorry so much that it has lost all meaning. He also says it quite flippantly.

When her son does something that warrants him saying sorry, he will say it, but she knows he doesn't mean it because he has grown up seeing it as a 'filler' word with no meaning.

Filler words also have a habit of sneaking into emails. Not only do we say these 'little words' but we write them without even thinking about it. Anastasia often started her emails with very tentative language. She was trying to be polite and not too direct but went too far so she looked weak instead.

A great tip is to re-read your emails before you send them specifically looking for 'little words'. Where can you change the words or remove them altogether?

Replacement ideas:

- Sorry for taking so long to reply → Thank you for your patience
- I'm just reaching out → I'm reaching out
- I think it's a good idea to → I believe we should
- Sorry to chase → Can you update me on

Re-read the last few emails you sent. Are there 'little words' that you overuse?

Retrain yourself to avoid these 'little words'. Re-reading emails is a great way to start because you get to review them before hitting send. It is time to start being deliberate about what you say and write.

You can take this into other communication, both written and verbal. You may not change instantly, but that is ok. However, the more deliberate you are with the words you use, by

- re-reading your emails to spot yourself;
- having a list of replacement phrases you'd like to use instead;
- deleting the 'little words' altogether;

the more you will create a brand-new habit of writing and talking without using 'little words'.

Once Neesha became aware that she was using language that had become meaningless for her son, she was able to choose different words to use instead. The less frequently she uses *sorry* unnecessarily, the more she breaks the cycle, so that in twenty years her son won't have to worry about the language he teaches his kids to use.

TOOL:

Before pressing send on an email, re-read it for 'little words' and replace or delete them.

Get deliberate with your language.

SORRY, THIS MAY BE A STUPID QUESTION

"Sorry, this may be a stupid question." Find yourself saying this one? Have you considered the knock-on impact of saying it? What does the other person think when you open your mouth to ask your (probably very insightful) question?

People in corporate say, "Sorry, this may be a stupid question," a lot. But one person stands out as saying it more than others. And that's Maria.

She was relatively new in the company. She had a complex role and had to understand lots of detail about how everything worked, so she could build a strategy and plan to improve what wasn't working and scale what was working. It was important that she asked lots of questions to understand what was really going on.

She had been there a few months when I heard her say, "Sorry, this may be a stupid question," at least three times in a meeting. However, they weren't stupid questions. She was new to the company.

Perhaps you have taken on a stretch project and are working in an area of the business you don't know much about. Maybe the person talking is overcomplicating things and using lots of acronyms and work jargon that no one else fully understands either.

I saw huge potential in Maria. However, every time she said, "Sorry, this may be a stupid question," she planted a thought in the other person's subconscious that the question she was about to ask was stupid. Remember, ninety-five percent of your thoughts are driven by your subconscious. It was as if she was saying, "Hey, I'm about to ask a stupid question, so you don't need to listen to me or take me seriously."

It was time for me to have a one-to-one conversation with Maria and give her feedback. (You can read more about giving and receiving feedback later on.)

I told her I had heard her apologise for asking stupid questions at least three times and I believed it had an impact on her credibility, when in fact, her questions were completely valid.

What she said next surprised me. She said, "But everyone else in the room is so smart. I feel lower than them all and that I don't deserve to be there."

Here's what we worked on together:

1. For her to become more aware of when she apologised.
2. She created some go-to phrases to use instead. For example, "Can I clarify?", "What does ABC mean?" or simply, "I have a question."
3. She figured out what her strengths were and used them more so she would no longer feel like she was lower than everyone else.

That conversation was about five years ago and Maria has changed so much. She recently told me, "It's no longer my go-to phrase. I still ask questions, but I don't apologise for it. I've gained back control of myself with more confidence so I no longer feel I need to apologise."

Do you say sorry for asking a stupid question? Like Maria, do you feel lower than others in the room, not smart enough, not good enough to be there, that you're winging it?

It is your inner critic who is scared that you may fail, look stupid or be judged. But remember, you also have an inner cheerleader.

I once heard a colleague say, "I'd rather ask a stupid question than make a stupid assumption."

We sometimes think a question is stupid because it is basic, yet it is worth going over the basics in order to get them right. Asking a basic question can be a great act of service to others, as well as clarification of something for yourself.

Ask the question and know that your question is valid. If you are thinking it, others probably are too.

FRAMEWORK:

Phrases you can use, in order to wipe, "Sorry, this may be a stupid question," from your vocabulary, include:

- "Can I clarify?"
- "What does ABC mean?"
- "I have a question."
- "Could you explain?"
- "Can you help me understand?"
- "I'm curious."

What phrases can you add to this list that feel good for you?

Tune into your inner critic. What do they want to remind you of?

Go for it and feel how much more powerful it is.

SORRY FOR INTERRUPTING!

You can interrupt someone without apologising but also without sounding rude.

Daniel is extremely smart. He spends a lot of time with numbers and data, and his inquisitive nature often leads him to interrupt people when they are talking, as he normally has insightful contributions to share.

But he has created a habit of saying, "Sorry to interrupt," because he doesn't want to come across as rude or arrogant.

Do you find it difficult to interrupt? Or do you automatically apologise for interrupting? Do you say, "Sorry for interrupting," or worse, do you have a great question to ask, but keep quiet because you worry about sounding rude.

It is worth understanding what stops you from speaking up, as we covered in Part One. Do you feel you don't deserve to be there? Do you feel you're not as smart as others in the room? Have you had feedback that you can be rude and aggressive?

Remember:

- You do deserve to be there.
- It isn't true that you're not smart enough.
- Your inner critic is trying to keep you safe.
- You can interrupt without sounding rude.

For over ten years now, I have worked with an amazing coach, Sarah Brummitt. One of the (many) things she has introduced me to is the 'elegant interruption'.

Before I share the tool, let's consider what happens if you don't interrupt elegantly. If you keep quiet altogether, your insight, question or input is never heard. If you do interrupt but in an inelegant way, you could come across as weak or rude. I'm sure none of this is your aim.

So how can you interrupt elegantly? Here is Sarah Brummitt's simple tool you can start using straight away.

1. Say their name.
2. Acknowledge that you're interrupting.
3. Make your point clearly.

For example:

1. Michael,
2. I'm interrupting
3. Because I want to clarify…

or

1. Amanda,
2. Can we pause for a moment?
3. I'd like us all to be clear on the actions for that section before we move on.

Simple, right? But also effective. Next time you want to interrupt someone, give it a try.

When Daniel tried this, he was blown away at how simple it was but also that people took him more seriously.

TOOL:

Elegant interruptions

1. Say their name.
2. Acknowledge that you are interrupting.
3. Make your point clearly.

YOU'RE TOO AGGRESSIVE

Perhaps you have been given advice or feedback that now means you apologise too much. Were you told you are too aggressive, too direct, too assertive?

Feedback can be great and some even say it's a gift… but only when it is given with positive intent. If someone gave you feedback because *they* want to feel better, or pay you back for annoying them, that is completely different from someone giving you feedback so you can grow and develop.

Often, we take feedback personally, but it is worth taking a moment to reflect on why the other person gave it to you. Was it given to you with positive intent?

Anastasia lives in England but grew up in Greece. Her culture is much more pragmatic and direct than the British culture.

Early on in her career she was given feedback from a boss that she was 'too direct' and people saw her as 'confrontational'. This wasn't what she had intended at all. Yes, she was direct, but that's how she was brought up.

She was young and impressionable and that feedback was from someone way more senior than her. She took it personally, believed she was doing it all wrong and had to fundamentally change who she was in order to be successful. She became conscious of not being too direct or confrontational and a new belief was formed that she wouldn't be successful if she was direct.

Fast forward twenty years, she heard the title of this book and told me it resonated with her because she apologises all the time.

When we unpicked it, she reflected that the feedback early on in her career had knocked her. She had pivoted because she didn't want people to think she was confrontational but she'd ended up over-correcting and now says sorry all the time. She says it before she asks a question, before she puts forward her ideas, before she speaks.

The feedback she'd been given resulted in her changing her natural style.

However, feedback often isn't even real. They are just sharing their opinion with you. Someone once told me that opinions are like bottoms. (Their language was much fruitier than mine.) Everyone has one but that doesn't mean we want to see them all!

Just because someone has an opinion, you don't necessarily have to listen to it and act on it. What feedback have you been given in the past? Was it genuine feedback given with positive intent? Or was it an opinion?

Did that feedback come from someone you respect? Would you proactively seek feedback from them? If not, perhaps take it with a pinch of salt.

This may be hard to do, but when you are given unsolicited feedback that wasn't given with positive intent, you don't have to accept it. You don't have to over-rotate like Anastasia did. You do not have to fundamentally change who you are.

The funny thing about receiving feedback (although it's not actually funny!) is that your brain is wired to have a negative bias.

You know from Part One that your brain and your subconscious are there to keep you safe. They are constantly on the lookout for danger, for things that are wrong and negative. They have a negative bias to keep you safe and the same happens when you hear feedback.

You probably remember the last bit of 'constructive' feedback you received but not necessarily the last positive feedback. You walk out of a review with your boss kicking yourself for the one piece of constructive feedback and completely forget all the positive things they told you at the same time.

Your brain holds onto the negative to keep you safe. I bet Anastasia's old boss gave her lots of positive feedback while she worked for him. But twenty years on, she only remembers that one piece of 'constructive' feedback.

Are you like Anastasia? Do you act and behave differently from who you naturally are because of some feedback given to you years ago?

Yes? Well done for being aware of it. Here's what can you do about it now.

EXERCISE:

— **Write down the feedback that has stuck with you and may result in you now apologising.**

— **Do you respect the person who gave you that feedback? Would you proactively ask for their feedback?**

— Challenge that feedback in your head. Is it true? Fair? Was it given with positive intent?

— How do you now act as a result of that feedback? Have you over-corrected?

— Ask someone you trust and respect what they think about the feedback. Do they see you doing it now? Have they noticed that you have over-corrected because of it?

— What do you choose to tell yourself and remind yourself of now?

SORRY VERSUS THANK YOU

I recently had a conversation with my teenage daughter. It started with me trying to teach her the value of money but ended up as a conversation encouraging her to stop apologising.

She wanted some new trainers, which we bought her. However, shoes for teenagers are not cheap. So, trying to teach her the value of money, when we gave them to her, I told her how much they cost so she would appreciate them and understand how expensive things are.

Her response was to say, "I'm sorry."

She was apologising for us having spent money on her. However, that wasn't my aim. The aim was for her to appreciate not apologise.

I said, "Please don't say sorry. You don't need to apologise; you can say thank you instead," to which she then apologised! Then she said, "Thank you."

Looking back at the stories so far, they all demonstrate times when we might apologise when it's not needed.

Neesha apologised for being late but then kept apologising and gave way too much information about why she was late. She also said, "Sorry for not getting back to you sooner," on email, even though it had only been a few hours, and for dinner being late. In fact, she apologised so much that the word *sorry* became meaningless.

Jada apologised when she cried and felt like she was taking up too much space. Maria apologised for asking a stupid question even though her questions were always insightful and valid. Daniel apologised for interrupting before he learnt about elegant interruptions. Anastasia filled her emails with 'little words' and apologised for everything, all the time, so she didn't come across as too aggressive and direct following feedback she received twenty years ago.

How about you? Which of these stories sound most like you?

TOOL:

Here are some replacement phrases to start using immediately when an apology or apologetic language isn't needed. There is space in the table for you to add your own 'go-to' phrases and replacements too.

Sorry.	Thank you.
Sorry for being late.	Thank you for your patience.
Sorry for being late, it's because of… Sorry!	Sorry for being late. (end of sentence)
Sorry, I know you're busy.	I appreciate your time. This is important.
Sorry to chase.	Can you update me on…?
Sorry, this may be a stupid question.	Can I clarify: what does ABC mean?
Sorry to interrupt.	Michael, I'm interrupting because I want to clarify…
Sorry dinner is late.	Dinner is ready.
Sorry for crying.	Thank you for holding space for me.
Sorry, I've just got a question.	I have a question.

CONSCIOUS COMPETENCE

I love, love, *love* this concept and my clients always do too.

You now have so much more awareness of what's stopping you, what beliefs you have that don't help you, how you sabotage yourself and what you could do differently. Awareness is great. However, are you now beating yourself up for some of this, thinking you are stupid or wrong (insert word of your choice here)?

You probably judge yourself for some of this, wishing you were different, thinking that you know this and you should do better. Quite simply, be kind to yourself and talk to yourself as you would talk to your best friend or a child.

To help you to be kind to yourself (as it is often easier said than done), here is a fabulous concept about conscious competence.

When we learn something new, whether to stop apologising, embrace a new belief or learn to drive, we go through four phases:

1. Unconscious incompetence.
2. Conscious incompetence.
3. Conscious competence.
4. Unconscious competence.

Take the example of learning to drive. Before you learn to drive you do not understand that you can't drive. You watch your parents drive and think, *this isn't so hard; I could do that.* You are unconsciously incompetent because you don't know how difficult it is to drive.

Reality hits you when you get behind the wheel for the first time. You don't know when to put your foot on the clutch, or when to change gear. You don't know how to coordinate looking in the mirror, indicating and turning the corner. You are now consciously incompetent.

After some lessons, you are able to drive but you have to think about *everything*: the engine revs, when to change gear, when to look in the mirror, checking your blind spot, etc. You are competent but you actively have to think about what you do and be conscious of every action you take. You are consciously competent.

Finally, once you have been driving for a while you reach the unconscious competence space. One day you realise you don't have to think about driving. You change gear because you know you need to change gear. You change lanes when you need to change lanes. You look in your blind spot without even thinking about it. Finally, after lots of practice you reach the final stage of unconscious competence.

In the early stages of conscious incompetence (the stage where you find it most difficult, because you realise you don't know what you're doing), you make a choice to either give up or keep practising. Most people keep up with the driving lessons because they know it will get easier and they have faith that soon they will become competent. Consider what you are learning now. How can you apply this principle?

With regard to apologising, you may have already been in the conscious incompetence space before picking up this book. You knew you apologised too much and you wished you didn't. Or perhaps you were unconsciously incompetent and it wasn't until you began reading that you realised how much of a habit it was and became aware of its impact.

By starting to put into practice all that you've learnt so far, you are probably in that beautiful space of conscious competence where you are learning and growing all the time. If so, congratulations. However, I can promise you that you will not stay in the conscious competence space forever. Firstly, as with learning to drive a car, it is not all smooth sailing even when you know the theory. You will have moments when you go straight back to the conscious incompetence space. The gears grind, the car bunny hops, you stall the car and your three-point turn takes twenty points even though you did it perfectly the day before!

The same is true for learning to stop apologising or embedding your new beliefs. There will be moments when you do it brilliantly and moments when you revert to the beginning.

You have a choice: either you throw in the towel and decide that you quit, that it's not working, give up, beat yourself up about it and judge yourself for it, or you can have faith that by practising and keeping at it, you *will* move to that wonderful unconscious competence space.

EXERCISE:

Take a moment to reflect on what you've learnt about yourself through reading this book.

— **List what you'd like to learn to do differently.**

— **Which stage of competency are you in for each?**

Remember to be kind to yourself knowing that you are on the right path to unconscious competence.

ASKING FOR FEEDBACK

In the earlier story, about how Anastasia was given feedback that she came across as being aggressive because her direct style went against the cultural norms in the UK, you were invited to consider when you have received unsolicited feedback and the impact it may have had on you and how you show up.

Asking for feedback and receiving feedback is great. I used to hate giving it and hated receiving it even more, especially if it was positive. I have grown to love giving and receiving feedback having seen how much can be gained from it.

When I was qualifying as a positive psychology coach, we were put in pods of three. Every week, we met and took turns coaching, being coached and observing. It has been proven that coaches improve not solely because of the hours they coach, but also by how much they reflect and how much feedback they seek.

Each week, after practising our positive psychology coaching in our pod, we gave each other feedback. We shared what each other did well and what they could consider doing more of or differently next time. I know I gave more constructive feedback than the others.

This went on week after week. After about five weeks, one of the coaches in my pod said that the first week I gave her feedback she was kind of upset that I had spotted something she could do differently. But after a couple of weeks, she looked forward to my feedback as she knew it would make her a better coach. Fast forward a few more weeks and she was spotting in herself the things she thought I would give her feedback on. She was growing massively each week.

As you can see, feedback really is a gift.

EXERCISE:

— What would you love to get feedback on? It could be that you are practising to sound more assertive or you want to get better at presenting and you'd love to know how you're getting on.

— Who would you like feedback from? Whose opinion do you value? Who will be honest with you? Who do you feel comfortable being vulnerable with?

Ask them! Using the framework and questions below.

Tell them the area you are developing and say you would value their feedback. Then ask:

1. What am I doing well that I should carry on doing?
2. What could I do to be even better?

When they give you their feedback, receive it with the positive intent that it is intended, take it on and see how you grow.

SUMMARY - STOP APOLOGISING STORIES

What are your takeaways from this collection of stories? Which stories did you love? What do you want to remind yourself of? Which tools will you put into practice?

In Your Apologising Rules the E is for *Establish your toolbox*. It is great to be inspired by stories, but it is key to establish your own toolbox with a collection of tools that you can start practising.

Below is a summary of the stories. Pause, read the summary, and perhaps look back to remind yourself of them. There is space below for you to write down your takeaways. If you write something down, you are five times more likely to remember it.

Which tools are going in your toolbox?

STOP APOLOGISING STORIES

Sorry for Not Replying Sooner

We heard Neesha apologise for being late (with all the details). She also said sorry for not replying to an email straight away, even though it had only been a few hours.

- It is ok to apologise when it is the polite thing to do.
- You don't need to keep saying sorry: once is fine.
- Say, "Thanks for your patience," instead of, "Sorry for not replying sooner."

Tool: Create a new habit of pausing to ask yourself "Do I need to apologise right now?"

Sorry Dinner Is Late

We heard Neesha say sorry for dinner being late, even though she was the only one who knew when she'd planned dinner for!

- Apologising unnecessarily plants a negative thought in the other person's head.
- It is often due to a habit you're not even consciously aware of.
- When you kick one habit, you build hope that you can kick even more.

Exercise: Write down when you habitually say sorry. What could you say instead? Start now.

Sorry for Crying

We heard Jada apologising when she cried. As a child she learnt to keep emotions contained.

- When you dig deep and reflect, emotions are normal.
- If you don't process your emotions, they can come out when you don't expect them to.
- All emotions are ok. Allow them so you can process them.

Remember: Allow tears to come. When a friend cries, resist the urge to tell them to stop. Hold space for them instead.

Sorry, but I've Just Got a Question

We heard Anastasia filling her emails with 'little words', repeatedly inserting the word *just*. Neesha apologised so much that it became meaningless in her house.

- Be mindful of 'little words' like *just*, *I think* and *probably*.
- Your words can become meaningless if overused.
- Spot filler words in emails.

Tool: Re-read recent emails for your 'little words'. Write a list of replacements and have them to hand when writing emails. Replace and delete before you hit send.

Sorry, This May Be a Stupid Question

We heard Maria apologising for asking a stupid question even though her questions were always insightful and valid. She felt she didn't deserve to be there.

- Saying, "Sorry, this may be a stupid question," is the equivalent of saying, "Hey, I'm about to ask a stupid question, so you don't need to listen to me or take me seriously."
- Over-apologising can impact your credibility.
- Your inner critic is trying to keep you safe so you don't look stupid, fail or be judged.

Framework: Tune into your inner critic. Why are you putting a precursor to your question? What do you want to remind yourself of instead?

Sorry for Interrupting!

We heard Daniel apologise for interrupting. He didn't want to come across as rude, which resulted in him coming across as weak instead.

- Do you apologise for interrupting or, even worse, stay quiet altogether?

- If you keep quiet, your insight, question or input is never heard.
- If you do interrupt but inelegantly, you could come across as weak or rude.

Tool: Elegant Interruptions.

1. Say their name.
2. Acknowledge that you are interrupting.
3. Make your point clearly.

You're Too Aggressive

We heard that Anastasia's feedback, received twenty years ago, resulted in her over-correcting, apologising so she wouldn't come across as too aggressive and direct.

- Your brain has a negative bias holding onto constructive feedback.
- Beliefs can be formed off the back of that feedback and result in over-pivoting.
- Opinions are like bottoms. Everyone's got one but you don't need to see it!

Exercise: Write down feedback you remember receiving. Is it true, fair and given by someone you respect? Have you over-pivoted?

Sorry Versus Thank You

I told you about my daughter saying sorry, instead of thank you, when I bought her new trainers.

- Be aware of when you say sorry.

- Ask yourself if sorry is needed.
- Have your list of go-to replacements.

Tool: Refer to the cheat sheet of replacements and add your own.

Conscious Competence

I illustrated the four phases by describing how people learn to drive. We don't go from knowing the theory of how to drive to driving like a racing driver instantly.

- When we become conscious, we can quickly beat ourselves up about it.
- Only through practice do we get more competent.
- If we keep at it, we become unconsciously competent.

Exercise: Be kind to yourself as you go through these four phases to stop apologising.

1. Unconscious incompetence.
2. Conscious incompetence.
3. Conscious competence.
4. Unconscious competence.

Asking for Feedback

I gave feedback to my fellow positive psychology coaches. Although it can feel uncomfortable, receiving feedback can help you grow.

- Remember, feedback is a gift.
- Think about what you would specifically love feedback

on.
- Seek feedback from those whose opinions you value.

Framework: Ask them two questions.

1. What am I doing well that I should carry on doing?
2. What could I do to be even better?

REFLECT

What are your takeaways from this collection of stories? What do you want to remind yourself of? Which tools are you going to put into practice first?

— Which tools and exercises do you love most?

CONFIDENCE STORIES

IT IS TIME TO CATAPULT YOUR CONFIDENCE

What would you do if you had more confidence? Would you go for that promotion? Ask for a pay rise? Start your own business? Talk up in meetings more? Put yourself out there and talk on stage?

Apologising too much and low confidence are closely linked. You may apologise as a way to seek validation, which people feel they need more of when they have lower confidence levels. If you don't feel confident, you are more likely to want to avoid conflict and rejection. Apologising could be your way to avoid them. The more self-doubt you have, the more you criticise yourself and second guess yourself, leading to more apologising.

In fact, apologising is a symptom of not feeling confident. When you feel confident, when you second guess yourself less, when you feel secure, when you make decisions driven by possibility instead of fear, you are far less likely to apologise unnecessarily.

You can start putting into practice the tools you have already learnt, but couple that with working on your confidence too, then you create an unstoppable upward spiral.

Helping you and others like you to catapult your confidence is the thing I love most about my job. In my recent group coaching program, one of my clients at the end of the program said they were ready to release any self-limiting beliefs, fears, judgement, doubt and second guessing themselves. They were ready to become a happier version of themselves, confident in being who they are. How amazing is that? In the following collection of confidence stories, I will give you more tangible tools and frameworks so that you can feel like this too.

You will hear more from the characters you met earlier, who are an amalgamation of real people I've coached, mentored and worked with over the years, as well as more of my own personal stories.

First, a question for you.

— **How would you score your confidence right now out of ten?**

One means you have no confidence. You doubt yourself all the time, you feel you're constantly apologising, you question yourself and are not sure what you are doing or why.

Ten means you feel great and you ooze confidence.

To help with your confidence, you'll now learn about Your Confidence Rules, with stories to bring each of the Rules to life. I created Your Rule Book™ so you can take the simple tools and apply them to your own life. We are all different, have different backgrounds and have experienced life differently so these Rules focus on helping you to reflect and grow in a way that feels good for you.

YOUR CONFIDENCE RULES

You can download Your Confidence Rules here: https://www.tararulecoaching.com/book-downloads and work through them as we go. There is also a video you can watch.

Your Confidence Rules are:

Remember what you are good at.
Use your strengths.
Large vision.
Exciting goals.
Strengthen with hope.

Let's take a moment to break each of them down.

Remember what you are good at. What are three of your strengths? Know what your strengths are, whether they're skills, qualities or characteristics. Knowing what you're good at and using those strengths will make you happier and more successful. I'll help you identify how you are unique and how to own your strengths.

Use your strengths. When can you use your strengths tomorrow? The more you use your strengths, the better you'll be, the more productive you'll be, the more energy you'll have, the more enthusiasm you'll have, and the more confident you'll feel. Turn your strengths into superpowers by using them more often.

Large vision. What excites you about your future? When you visualise something, it influences your subconscious, making you feel more motivated, focused and confident. You're much more likely to achieve it if you've envisioned it. Get excited about what is possible, what your best possible life looks like and go after it with a new, fun energy.

Exciting goals. What do you want to give ten out of ten to? When you achieve goals, you feel a sense of accomplishment. You have more hope for the future and you feel more confident and optimistic for what might be coming. Set yourself some goals that excite you, that you want to achieve and see how far you can fly.

Strengthen with hope. What is true and positive for you? When you have more hope, you gain increased job satisfaction, increased happiness, more resilience, increased performance, and less anxiety. Who wants some of that? Talk to yourself as if you were talking to your best friend and start believing.

YOU ARE NOT ALONE

Before you go deeper into Your Confidence Rules, remember you are not alone! Not in an alien sense but in the sense that you may feel you are the only one who doesn't feel confident, doubts themselves, hates presenting, gets nervous talking in meetings or whatever your inner critic is telling you that you can't do.

I asked everyone in my group coaching program recently what they love most about the group and one said, "I've realised that I'm not alone in the way I feel and that opening up doesn't have to be hard." I love that I've created a safe space where people can share their inner fears knowing they won't be judged but also learning that they're not alone.

I recently spoke to an ex-colleague who had just started her new role as Chief Marketing Officer. As you can imagine, having the word 'Chief' in the title means it was a big job. Which it was. You would also imagine that she was good at what she did and she had the right experience to have been offered this role. Again, you're right. You therefore may imagine that she was confident she would do a great job. Wrong! Even though she had years of experience, was more than qualified for the role and had demonstrated in the long and intensive interview process that she was right for the job, when we spoke, she said she had massive imposter syndrome and wondered if she could do it.

It is so easy to feel isolated in your own world of lacking confidence. I can't stress enough that it doesn't matter whether you're starting out in your career or if you've already got the word Chief in your job title, we all have moments when our inner critic jumps up and down and impacts our confidence. You don't have to let the inner critic win and stay safe by saying no when opportunities arise.

Have hope that there are so many people doing what you want to do, whether that's presenting, getting the big job, or starting their own business who once felt like you do. Nothing you dream of is impossible.

"IT ALWAYS SEEMS IMPOSSIBLE UNTIL IT'S DONE."

- Nelson Mandela

Knowing you are not alone:

— **What do you want to say yes to?**

— **What do you want to remind yourself of?**

R — REMEMBER WHAT YOU ARE GOOD AT

The first and crucial step to catapult your confidence is to remember what you are good at. In other words, what are your strengths?

Did you know that only a third of people know what their strengths are? I was shocked when I first heard this statistic a few years ago so I did a poll on social media asking the simple question: *Do you know your strengths?* Only twenty-seven percent voted Yes.

This matters because research shows that when you know your strengths *and* use them, you are happier and more successful… and therefore, more confident.

Ever done a strengths survey? Perhaps you have done one as part of a team meeting. Strengths Finder, VIA Strengths and Marcus Buckingham are popular ones. I encourage my clients to do VIA Strengths. It is free but also gives a slightly different perspective as it looks at your character strengths instead of the more traditional skills strengths.

You may have done one or many of these surveys, but do you still remember what they said? Would you need to root around to find where you wrote them down?

Some of my strengths are: positivity, coaching, simplifying the complex, honesty, being genuine, building relationships, telling a story through numbers, creating a strategy, engaging people, listening, kindness, bringing the best out of people, running workshops, hope, relating with people. Also, I often joke with my clients that my superpower is making people cry!

When I started writing this book, I wrote down my why – as in, why I was writing this book. My why was to positively impact millions of people, whether by a person reading it and feeling more confident afterwards, by a reader contacting me to run a workshop at their company, or simply by you sharing a snippet from this book with a friend.

I also wrote down my strengths that I planned to use when writing, including simplifying the complex, making it relatable and easy for people to apply, positivity and the fact that I've worked through all this myself so I knew I was writing from experience. I wrote these down and stuck them to my office wall, so I remembered them every time I wrote.

Identify your strengths, get to know them and yourself more, then choose three that resonate with you the most. The next three stories will help you with this.

OWN THEM!

Neesha was taking part in my group coaching program. One of the modules is all about Your Strengths. She found this module hard. She had done her VIA strengths survey, she was listening to what I was saying and understood the importance of knowing her strengths, but she couldn't say what hers were. She felt uncomfortable 'owning them'.

When I asked her what the survey said her strengths were, she told me they were kindness, appreciation and curiosity. When I asked her what feedback she'd been given from her peers and her boss and old bosses, she told me they had said she was analytical, supportive and calm. But she then said, "But these are nothing special; they're just things that I do."

That's it, though! Your strengths are just things you're good at and you find easy, things that come naturally to you that you don't need to think about.

You may find them easy, but that doesn't mean everyone else does. Neesha finds it easy to be analytical, but that doesn't mean that I do or you do. It is unique to her when combined with her other strengths of curiosity and being calm.

What comes naturally to you? It could be creativity, being analytical, compassion, relationship building, getting the most out of people, storytelling, positivity, or your energy. They don't all have to be hard skills; think about yourself as a fully rounded person. When do you feel comfortable and in flow, when time flies by? Think about when you're at work, but also when you're at home or with friends.

Here are some words to inspire you to think about your strengths.

Assertive	Adaptable	Energetic	Relationships	Leader
Trustworthy	Adventurous	Caring	Creative	Consistent
Inclusive	Calm	Takes Action	Collaborative	Credible
Approachable	Positive	Mindful	Direct	Innovative
Challenger	Smart	Genuine	Eloquent	Fun
Imaginative	Resilient	Motivated	Logical	Driven

EXERCISE:

What are your strengths? List as many words as you can, aiming for at least ten.

Think about feedback you have received in the past. What do you find easy? What do others come to you for help with? What resonates with you from surveys you've done in the past?

— **What are your strengths?**

Circle the three strengths that mean the most to you.

Which ones do you find easy, love using or doing, and make you who you are?

PHONE A FRIEND

Perhaps you find it hard to think of your strengths, so here's another approach which could help you. Even if you found the last exercise easy, you'll still love this.

Daniel is very self-aware but downplays his strengths. However, when you use your strengths, you start that upwards spiral. You feel better about yourself, are more successful, more confident and happier.

I set him a challenge: "Send three messages. One to a colleague, another to a family member and one to a friend. Say that you're looking at your strengths and you'd love to know what they think are your top three strengths."

Daniel's best friend had recently been going through a tough situation at home. What happened next was lovely. Daniel's friend replied and also used it as an opportunity to say thank you for being by his side and supporting him in his time of need.

Without that prompt, his friend may never have said how much he appreciated Daniel. That one message created a fantastic ripple effect of positivity.

EXERCISE:

Stop right now, put this book down, pause your audiobook and send three messages. One to a colleague, another to a family member and the last one to a friend of yours. Say that you're looking at your strengths and you'd love to know what they think your top three strengths are.

Do it now!

How did that feel? What did they say? Did their reply resonate? Did they say something you've never thought about before? Did they confirm what you thought too?

— **Write down the words that they said.**

Take a moment to go back to the last exercise. Are there any new words you would add to your list of strengths?

UGH. DON'T THEY LOVE THEMSELVES?

Since when did it become a bad thing to love yourself?

You know what I mean: we see someone on social media being confident and we say or hear, "Ugh, don't they love themselves!" We see someone walking down the road dressed flamboyantly and full of confidence and people think they're trying to be the centre of attention. Society judges them more than celebrates them. When you think about it, it is sad.

It wasn't always this way. A toddler or a very young child being the centre of attention is seen as a great thing. Everyone cheers when they wave, clap or take their first steps. They are loving life, feeling and acting confidently and it is celebrated. But fast forward a few years, and they hear, "Don't be a show off" or, "Stop trying to be the centre of attention," and, "Shh, be quiet." They learn not to draw attention to themselves, not to appear overly confident and not to love themselves. Fast forward a few more years and that child judges other people for loving themselves too. I'd bet that most of you reading this would find it really hard to say, "I love myself," and mean it.

As you grow up, you no longer feel like that toddler. You are not cheered on by everyone, you are not happy being the centre of attention, you no longer love yourself and you no longer feel confident.

Imagine a world where you did love yourself. Where your best friend knew how amazing they were and loved themselves, where your partner looked in the mirror and said they loved themselves as much as you love them, where your work besties feel confident and love themselves too.

Not in an arrogant 'I'm better than you' way, but in an inward 'I love who I am' way. Would the world be better, kinder, happier? I think so!

Here is an exercise for you to try. It is up to you if you write these down, say them out loud to yourself or to another person or simply think them in your head.

> — **What is one thing you love about another person? Could be your partner, your child or a friend.**

> — **What is one thing you love about your life?**

How are you finding those so far? Ok?

> — **What is one thing you love about yourself?**

I hope you are thinking, what, only one thing? How could I possibly choose? But from my many years' experience coaching, the odds are that you are currently squirming in your seat finding it hard to come up with one.

But please do it. Think of one thing that you love about yourself.

Lucy's mum told me that she did this exercise with her daughter. They often say three things they are grateful for when they have dinner so Lucy is used to answering questions like this.

"What's one thing you love about me?" her mum said.
"Your hugs," said Lucy straight away.
"Ah, thank you. And what's one thing you love about your life?"
"I have a comfy bed," was the reply after a bit more thought.

"Nice. And what's one thing you love about yourself?"
"Ugh, Mum! Don't be weird! I don't know!"

At such a young age Lucy already feels uncomfortable thinking about and declaring what she loves about herself. Most adult clients find this exercise hard too.

I am going to push you one step further and ask you:

What are three things you love about yourself?

It could be a quality you have like being a good friend, that you're funny or honest.
Maybe it is a skill you have like being a good cook or listener, or that you're creative.
Perhaps it is a physical quality like your hair, your toned muscles or your smile.

Have a think and don't be shy.

— **What are three things you love about yourself?**

The more you love yourself from within, the more your confidence will grow. The next time you see someone else who loves themselves, celebrate it as it is so rare.

EXERCISE:

You can do this by yourself or with someone you love and say it together.

Say what you love about another person.
Say what you love about your life.
Say what you love about yourself.

A word of warning. If you have young children and decide to ask them what they love about themselves, while some may find it easy, most will find it hard and won't know what to say. That is ok. Be kind to them, but also be kind to yourself as their parent. The fact that you are asking them is great. I was forty before I asked myself this question and I found it hard then, so asking them at a young age is great and you are helping them to be way ahead of me!

SUMMARY - REMEMBER WHAT YOU ARE GOOD AT

The first step (I would say the most important) to feeling more confident to be yourself, is to remember what you are good at. If you don't know what you're good at, you can't do what you're good at; if you don't do what you're good at, it is much harder to accomplish anything; if you don't feel like you are accomplishing anything, it is much harder to feel confident. Remembering what you're good at is the catalyst that starts it all.

Know what your strengths are, whether they are skills, qualities or characteristics. Knowing what you're good at and using those strengths will make you happier and more successful.

The exercises we just went through that can help you are:

1. Write down all your strengths and circle those that resonate most with you.
2. Ask a colleague, family member and friend what they think your strengths are.
3. Think about what you love about yourself.

To help you to Remember what you are good at, write down:

— **What are three of your strengths?**

U — USE YOUR STRENGTHS

Well done for discovering a bit more about your strengths and what you are good at.

The next step to catapult your confidence is to Use Your Strengths. It is great to know what you're good at, but *doing* what you're good at is a massive unlock.

The more you use your strengths, the better you'll be, the more productive you'll be, the more energy you'll have, the more enthusiasm you'll have, and the more confident you'll feel.

Imagine the upward spiral you create by starting to use your strengths more.

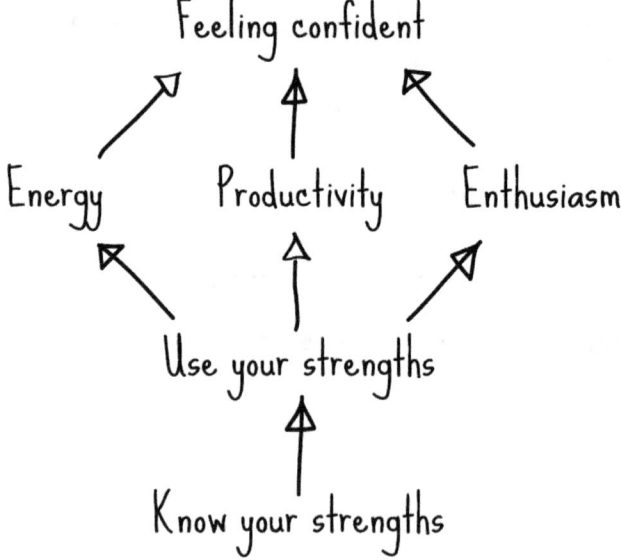

WHO WANTS TO BE A CIRCLE? NOT ME!

We often spend a lot of time working on our development areas, but what if we play to our strengths instead?

When Lucy was at primary school, she had a spelling test every week. She came home and her mum asked how she had got on with her spelling test. She might say, "I got nine out of ten."

What do you think her mum said to that? Either, "Well done, that's fantastic," and leave it at that, or do you think she said, "Ooh, which one did you get wrong?"

What would you say? What did your parents say to you?

So often we focus on the one we get wrong instead of the nine we get right. Schools often put a huge focus on your development areas and what you 'must try harder' at.

Then you start working, like Maria did, and people carry on focussing on your development areas. When Maria started working in her corporate job her boss would have a review with her every three months where he told her where she needed to focus. She needed to get better at presenting. She needed to be more assertive. She needed to improve her PowerPoint skills.

Have you had similar reviews? How does it feel to always have someone pointing out where you could try harder and what you need to improve? Not great, is it?

I'd like you to now think of yourself as a star! (Bear with me!)

You are a star. You have pointy bits and you have inner bits. Your pointy bits are your strengths and your inner bits – the inner angles – are your development areas. Similar to a line on a graph that goes up and down, none of us are equally good at every single thing we do. We are not flat lines.

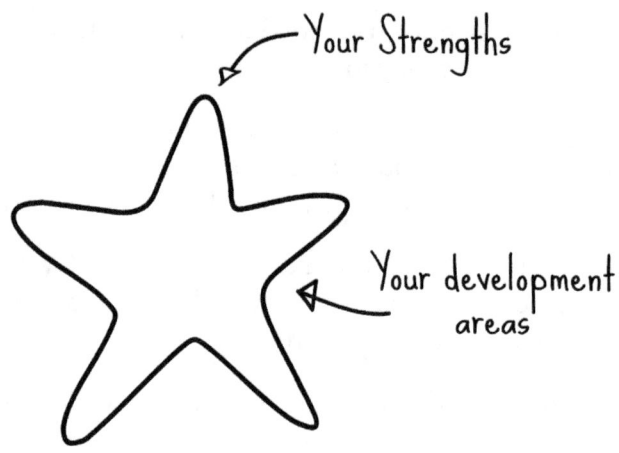

We all have pointy bits and we all have inner bits!

What was Lucy's mum trying to do when she focussed on which spelling she got wrong? What does the school system try to do? What was Maria's boss trying to do when he focussed on what she needed to improve?

Trying to help, yes, but also trying to turn us into circles!

If you spend all your time working on your development areas, you will probably get better at them, but the inner bits (development areas) of the star will move further out towards the points (your strengths). In the end, you will no longer be a star: you'll be a circle!

But who wants to be a circle?

Think about what happens if you spend more time on your strengths instead.

You can develop your strengths by reading books or listening to podcasts about things you enjoy and are naturally good at.

When I listen to something I already know the foundations of, I love it when I learn a nugget I didn't know before that will elevate me further.

A few years ago I knew I wanted to continue to build on my strength of coaching. I decided to earn another coaching qualification but I wasn't sure what. I then heard about positive psychology coaching. This built on three of my strengths: positivity, coaching and my curiosity about how our brains work, so I knew it was a perfect fit. Not only did I love doing the course, it also meant those strengths became even stronger because I had spent time developing them.

It is not about never working on your development areas but spending way more time playing to your strengths.

If you spend more time developing and using your strengths, those pointy bits get bigger and pointier and move further and further out. Your strengths become superpowers. Imagine how brightly you will shine!

— Do you want to be a circle or a star?

EXERCISE:

— Which of your strengths would you love to develop even further?

— How can you develop them? e.g. listening to podcasts, reading books, courses, qualifications.

Spend time focussing on your strengths and see how brightly you can shine.

USE YOUR STRENGTHS OFTEN

I hope that by now you know what some of your strengths are. Remind yourself of the previous section of 'Remember What You Are Good At'. In fact, you may want to look back at that page every day until it becomes natural to talk and think about your strengths.

You are also choosing to be a star! Spend more time developing your strengths than anything else.

Think about how often you actually use your strengths.

Choose three of your strengths and do this exercise for each of them.

Have you used that strength in the last year?
Have you used that strength in the last three months?
Have you used that strength in the last month?
Have you used that strength in the last week?
Have you used that strength in the last day?
Have you used that strength in the last hour?

A year ago, I did this exercise whilst running an Unlock Your Superpower workshop for a women's network.

Having already done an exercise to help people think about their strengths, I asked everyone to stand up. "Stay standing if you have used your strengths within the last year," I said and the whole room smiled and stayed standing.

"The last three months," I said. Again, I had a room full of standing people but a few nervous laughs.

"The last month." This was when people started looking around and started to sit down.

"The last week." Half the room was now seated.

"The last day." Only a few were still standing.

"And stay standing if you've used that strength in the last hour." We were left with only one person still standing. And lots of laughter in the room.

If you want to be a star, think about how you can use your strengths every single hour of every single day.

A great tip for when you are doing something you find hard or that is part of your job you don't enjoy, is to ask yourself, "How can I use one of my strengths while I'm...." (Insert the thing you don't want to do, i.e. creating the spreadsheet, doing my expenses, replying to emails, hoovering, etc.)

You always have a way to use one of your strengths while doing the things you don't like. I often talk to my clients about how they can use their strengths more and I have heard so many great ideas.

Some people make it a game to see how many emails they can reply to in thirty minutes using their strength of making things fun, others use their strength of appreciation when updating a deal tracker, appreciating that they have so many potential clients that tracking them takes so long! Others listen to a podcast while cleaning, playing to their strength of loving to learn.

EXERCISE:

— What do you find difficult or don't enjoy doing?

— What strengths can you use when doing it?

Have a play and I challenge you to think a bit differently. See if you can make that task a bit more enjoyable by using your strengths.

CONGRATULATIONS, YOU SMASHED IT THIS WEEK

This is the title of an email you could send yourself every single week (like I used to). I sent it to myself every Friday for eighteen months and it absolutely boosted my confidence.

Knowing your strengths and using them isn't always easy. If you are prepared to try, as I know you are, let's also celebrate that you are using them. Celebrate what you are doing well, how you are growing, feedback you've received and the impact you are making.

I often share this idea with my group and one-to-one clients and it is a winner that people love.

All you need to do is send yourself an email with the title: *Congratulations (insert your name), you smashed it this week!*

In that email put today's date and at least one thing you are proud of this week.

Consider these questions to help you write your email:

- What strengths have you used this week?
- What have you ticked off your to-do list?
- What meetings have you had? Which do you feel went well and why?
- What are you glad that you prioritised?
- What feedback have you had from others?
- What do you feel proud of?

You could write one thing or ten. It doesn't matter, but it's a great habit to start.

You are training your brain to look back at the week and feel a sense of accomplishment. When you experience feelings of accomplishment, you build hope for the future and you feel more confident about what you can achieve.

Then next week, do it again! Find that email, hit reply, add the date and again write at least one thing you're proud of that week.

Put a reminder in your diary so you remember to do it every week. Fifteen minutes on a Friday afternoon is perfect. But choose a time and day that works for you. Watch your self-awareness increase, have that feeling of accomplishment ooze into your life and see your confidence grow.

EXERCISE:

Stop right now and create that first email. Don't overthink it. Write one thing that you're proud of and hit send.

Put a reminder in your diary to email yourself next week too.

SUMMARY - USE YOUR STRENGTHS

Using your strengths creates an amazing upward cycle.

The more you use your strengths, the better you'll be, the more productive you'll be, the more energy you'll have, the more enthusiasm you'll have, and the better and more confident you'll feel.

The exercises we went through that can help you are:

1. Decide to be a star not a circle. Turn your strengths into superpowers so you can shine.
2. How often do you use your strengths? When can you lean on your strengths more for the stuff you don't enjoy doing?
3. Start celebrating what you're proud of and when you've used your strengths, by sending yourself a weekly email.

To help you to Use your strengths. Write down:

— **When can you use your strengths tomorrow?**

L — LARGE VISION

The third step in Your Confidence Rules is to aim for something big. A purpose. A vision. Something you believe in and can envision.

Perhaps it is something you have half thought about that is both scary and exciting (like standing on a TED stage), something that feels indulgent (like being on a yacht), something to do with your family (Christmas dinner surrounded by happy kids that haven't been born yet) or something that will make the world a better place (like starting up your own charity). It doesn't matter what it is, but having something exciting to aim for and believing it is possible can give your confidence a big boost.

Please don't underestimate the power of belief.

"WHETHER YOU THINK YOU CAN, OR YOU THINK YOU CAN'T - YOU'RE RIGHT."

- Henry Ford

If you believe you are going to have a rubbish day, that you won't achieve that dream life you dare not think about, then you won't.

But what if you believe you are going to have a great day and you'll achieve all of your dreams?

You have probably heard the term manifesting before. I see it as thinking something will happen, believing it will happen and it then happening. I believe there is a final step that is crucial, which is taking inspired action instead of sitting back and waiting for it to happen.

Manifesting
(verb)
the act of bringing something into your life through belief.

Here are my three steps for manifesting:

1. You have a vision.
2. You believe it will happen.
3. You take inspired action.

Let's take an example of changing careers.

First, have that vision to start with, i.e. to change your career, to do something you love where you use your strengths, and feel happy and confident.

Then, know and believe it will happen. This does not mean only *thinking* it will happen, but instead having the unwavering *belief* that it will, even if you don't know how. Believe it is just around the corner, that you deserve it, and that you will succeed. When you have that belief, you are far more likely to take inspired action to make it happen.

With this true belief that you will change careers, you are more likely to see opportunities you have not noticed before and to take more inspired action. You will take more inspired action when you have that belief that it will all work out. When looking to change careers the inspired action you may take includes researching different roles, signing up for a course, finding a mentor, applying for roles, etc.

All this starts with the first step of a large vision and aiming for something. Visualising this helps you build hope and boosts your confidence.

Earlier, we explored how your brain works and learned that you have sixty thousand thoughts every single day, with ninety-five percent coming from your subconscious. When you visualise something, it influences your subconscious, making you feel more motivated, focused and confident, impacting both your beliefs and behaviours.

You may have heard about athletes who close their eyes and visualise the ball going in the hole or basket before they take their shot. Their brains have been influenced to believe it can happen because they have just seen it.

Once you have a large vision, you start to believe it and feel more confident that your dreams are possible.

Ready to try it?

LET'S GET VISUALISING

You may be thinking, "Yes! I know what my vision is." You may have an idea… or maybe nothing comes to mind.

All of these and everything in between is ok. You are exactly where you are meant to be. To help you, I will invite you to visualise your future for a few moments.

If you are listening to this on audiobook, close your eyes and allow yourself to visualise as I talk (as long as you're not driving, of course!)

Reading this? Then read the whole thing, then pause for a few minutes and re-read it, allowing yourself space to shut your eyes and reflect after each line.

Alternatively, feel free to check out a recording of this visualisation at:
https://www.tararulecoaching.com/book-downloads

Ready? Take a deep breath in. And out. Again, a deep breath in. And out. And finally, one more deep breath in. And out.

I invite you to come to this with love, kindness and gratitude.

Now imagine you in the future. Your best possible future. The best possible you.
It may be next week, next year or in ten years, it doesn't matter. Imagine feeling confident, strong and full of energy.
Picture a future where you feel good and energised.
You're feeling the best you've ever felt.
Your health is strong.
You have great relationships with those around you, with friends, family or colleagues.
You feel happy and successful.
You've accomplished what you wanted.
You feel excited imagining this future.

You feel confident.
You feel energised.
Call up this vision of your future.
What do you look like?
How do you feel?
What are you doing?
How are you standing or seated?
Where are you?
Who are you with?
What's your routine?
How do you feel?
How does it feel to be happy, confident and energised?

Take a few moments to envision that future version of you and when you're ready, sit up straight, smile and open your eyes.

EXERCISE:

— **Take a few minutes to write down what came up for you.**

— **How did the visualisation feel?**

— **What are you excited about when you think of your future?**

Remember, you're so much more likely to achieve something once you've visualised it. Keep picturing that future of yours, keep believing, keep taking inspired action and know that your perfect future is possible.

Is there an object, an image, a word, or a visual that represents your vision? For me, it is a sunhat; for clients of mine it has been images of a sunset, a picture of them on the beach with their dog, running shoes, a shell, or a necklace.

If you have an image or object that represents your vision, place it somewhere you will see it often so that your brain is prompted to remember that visualisation regularly. I bought a sunhat and put it in my office so that my brain would be reminded of my visualisation every day. You may need to print off a picture, draw something, or find the object that is right for you.

WHY? WHY? WHY?

If you are a parent, how often do you hear this word? All the time, right?

As we grow older, we stop asking why. Simon Sinek has a great TED Talk called *'Start with Why - How great leaders inspire action'*. He talks about the power of a company knowing their why and says that companies which start with their why are much more successful.

What about your why?

You are much more likely to hit your goals and your vision if you know your why. How often do you feel motivated right after you set a goal, but then things get hard, the motivation wanes and you give up? What's missing is knowing your why. So many people miss out this key step.

Think of your vision from earlier. What did you picture?

Were you on a beach?
Were you feeling fit and healthy?
Were you running your own business?

Why is this vision important to you?

If you were on a beach, your why could be that you want a future where your job allows you to travel the world and see amazing sights.

If you were feeling fit and healthy, why is this important? Do you want to set a good example for your kids or is it so you live a long healthy life?

If you were running your own business, why is this important to you? Are you looking for financial freedom, independence, a better balance, to make a bigger difference?

Here is why I set up my business.

It all started years ago, back in 2015 when I wrote my first blog. (You can check it out at cocktailsandcoaching.blogspot.com) I wrote that blog, not caring how many people read it or how many likes I got. I had one purpose. That was to positively impact one person. It was great, because I knew why I wrote each entry: to inspire someone. It also meant I didn't put a huge amount of pressure on myself for vanity metrics.

As the years went on, I realised I could impact hundreds of people through my blog, my coaching and my workshops.

When I started working with my own coaches back in 2021, I shared that my why was to positively impact thousands of people. My core why doesn't change, only the number of people I want to impact has grown.

When I started writing this book and met with my publisher, I told her my purpose was to positively impact tens of thousands of people and she challenged me to increase it even further to millions. Sat in my office typing, on a cold and dark January afternoon, I can share with you that my why, my purpose, my large vision, is to positively impact the world. I know I can do that one by one!

That might be through you reading this book and feeling more confident than before you started, coaching someone so they believe they are good enough, being a role model that inspires someone to believe they too can be a good, decent human being *and* a strong leader, or helping someone realise their dream of starting their own business.

It is funny, but as I have been typing this, I've been sent a message from someone on LinkedIn saying, "You don't know me, but we used to work together and I would like to say you are an inspiration." How amazing is that? I am crystal clear on my why, my large vision and I am living proof that you can make it a reality when you believe and take inspired action.

EXERCISE:

— **What did you see in your visualisation?**

— **Why is it important to you?**

— **What is your why?**

LET'S RELEASE THE PRESSURE

You're probably in one of two camps regarding that last part about knowing your why and spending time visualising your future.

Either you feel inspired, clearer now on your why than you've ever been before and excited for all that's possible for you. Or you feel a little deflated, overwhelmed and still no clearer on your why. Either of those and anything in between is absolutely fine. We are all on our own journey and life is not a competition.

When I delivered a workshop to a room of sixty leaders at Amazon on Work Life Harmony last year, someone in the audience asked me about knowing your purpose. She said she's heard a lot about purpose and didn't know hers. It also sounded like she was putting a lot of pressure on herself to find hers and she asked me when I found mine. My answer was that I was already in my forties when I felt a strong sense of my purpose, to positively impact the world, with a clear path of how I could achieve it.

If you find all this talk about purpose, vision and finding your why difficult, please take a deep breath. Smile. Relax. Allow yourself to let go of any pressure.

EXERCISE:

Remember that life is not a race.

Relax and let go of any pressure you are putting on yourself.

Instead, simply allow yourself to dream about it and think about what excites you about your future.

SUMMARY - LARGE VISION

You are much more likely to achieve a goal when you envision it. Visualisations influence your subconscious making you feel more motivated, focused and confident.

Manifesting at its best is made up of three steps.

1. You have a vision.
2. You believe it will happen.
3. You take inspired action.

But having a vision is the first step.

The exercises we went through that can help you are:

1. Visualise your best possible future, your best possible you.
2. Think about your why.
3. Release the pressure if you find it difficult.

To help you to have a Large vision, write down:

— **What excites you about your future?**

E — EXCITING GOALS

The fourth step in your Confidence Rules is to set some exciting goals.

Not setting a goal you think you *should* set.
Not setting a goal you will beat yourself up about every day because you've not yet achieved it.
And not setting a goal other people think you should aim for.

Set goals that excite you, that you want to put your time and energy into, that you feel motivated to achieve.

Are you the kind of person who loves setting goals? Or do you hate setting them?

Personally, I love setting goals (but I never used to).

"IF YOU AIM AT NOTHING, YOU'LL HIT NOTHING."

- Zig Ziglar

Why is goal setting important? Research shows that:

1. A key part of our happiness and wellbeing comes from being able to look back at life and feel a sense of accomplishment.
2. Working towards goals helps us build hope for the future.
3. When we look back at past successes and goals we've

reached, we feel more confident and optimistic for the future.

A huge step towards confidence is feeling a sense of achievement, but it is hard to feel like you've achieved anything unless you actually have goals you are working towards in the first place.

You will also get more than you bargained for (in a good way). We often don't set goals because of the fear of the unknown but as you reach for your goals you will see new opportunities, have new insights and grow even further.

Aim at something that excites you and imagine what could happen for you.

COULDA SHOULDA WOULDA

What kind of goals do you set for yourself?

Do you have goals (or things on your to-do list) that:

- You feel you *should* do?
- You feel you *could* do?
- You *would* do *if* the circumstances were different?
- You think *others* want you to do?

It is so easy to fall into the trap of setting goals, having ambitions, having things on your to-do list that are a combination of the above.

But… what do you *want* to do? I mean what do you *really* want to do? What do you want to give ten out of ten to?

If you try to do everything, at most you'll give everything a seven out of ten. Perhaps even less. Life is too short for a whole bunch of sevens.

Here is an interaction that Lucy had with her mum a few years ago.

Lucy wasn't sure if she wanted to carry on going to dance class after school. She was finding it hard to decide. There were reasons to carry on and reasons to stop.

Her mum asked her to write down all the things she could do after school. Like going to dance class, hockey or football. What things did she feel she *had* to do? Homework was added to the list. What about what she felt *others* thought she should do? Dance came up on this list for her. And what did *she* want to do? Chill in her room.

She only had a certain number of hours in a week so her mum asked her to decide what things she really wanted to give ten out of ten to.

She listed three things instantly. Hockey, football and chilling. Unfortunately, homework couldn't be kicked off the list all together, much to her annoyance! However, dance was the obvious one she didn't want to give ten out of ten to.

And that was ok. She had been dancing for years, but that didn't mean she had to carry on; it was time to stop. She didn't need to feel guilty or apologise for it. It was ok for her to decide to stop. By stopping, she freed up more time for the things she loved whether that was other clubs or chilling in her room.

Where do you feel like you are trying to do everything, but only giving anything a seven out of ten?

EXERCISE:

Write down everything you think you *could* do, *should* do and *others* want you to do.

Think about your big goals in life. Add your goals from the four quadrants that I think about when setting goals, which are personal, financial, health and career/business.

You may want to look at your to-do list, think about your extra-curricular activities like going to the gym, swimming and meeting with friends. Write them all down now.

— **Write your list here:**

Take another look and circle the things you *want* to do, and you want to give ten out of ten to. These are the things that will excite you, you will go the extra mile for, put the effort in to achieve and enjoy doing along the way.

As for the rest of it? Choose to give them a zero. It may be a zero for today only, or it may be a zero forever. You may need to say no to something or someone. That is ok. Trying to give everything a seven won't make you happy and will mean you don't do any of it well.

— **What are your ten out of ten goals?**

YOUR COMFORT ZONE IS LIKE KNICKER ELASTIC

How often do you put yourself out there, take a risk or step outside of your comfort zone?

Every day? Every week? Every month? Or are you thinking, never!

Most people are very happy doing what they've always done. Not really challenging themselves, not doing something they may fail at, not saying yes to talking on stage, not going for a big promotion, not starting their own business. Why? Because fear is a strong emotion that drives our decisions and actions, even when we're not aware of it. This leads to most people staying firmly in their comfort zone most of the time.

If you always stay in your comfort zone, how can you grow, develop and feel more confident?

> **Insanity**
> *(noun)*
> doing the same thing over and over and expecting different results. - *Albert Einstein*

Imagine your comfort zone being inside two other zones. You can think of them as three concentric circles.

The first, inner circle is your comfort zone. Just outside is your stretch zone and further out you have your panic zone.

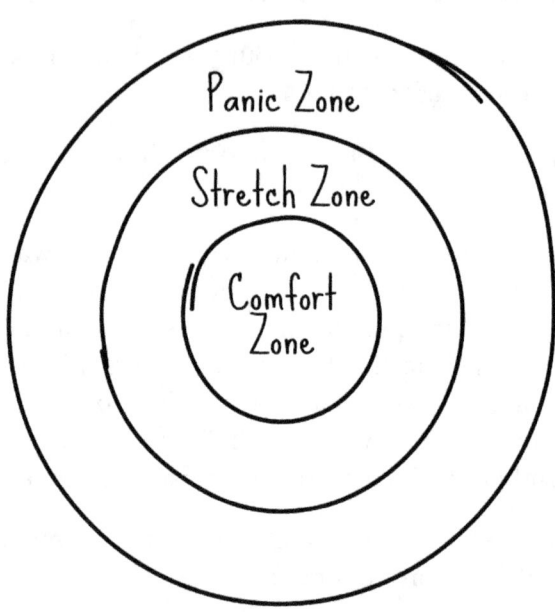

Beth is an experienced nanny, having cared for children of various ages, but she had a fear of public speaking. Apparently, the fear of public speaking is a fear greater than death for most people, so I expect this will sound familiar to you to some degree.

COMFORT ZONE

Beth was in her comfort zone looking after children, talking to other nannies about her job and the children she looked after and discussing the day-to-day with the children's parents. Most of the time she was quite comfortable in the inner circle, her comfort zone.

You may feel comfortable having conversations with peers and your boss about your day-to-day work.

STRETCH ZONE

When she felt she needed to have a more difficult conversation with her boss about the kids' behaviour she moved into the stretch zone. She didn't like having a conversation which could be seen as confrontational, even though she knew exactly what she was talking about.

You many need to have a difficult conversation or lead a discussion in a team meeting with a wider audience and this may push you slightly into the next circle of your stretch zone.

PANIC ZONE

Finally, Beth was pushed way into her panic zone when she was asked to go to her old school and talk to a group of sixteen and seventeen-year-olds who were considering a career in childcare. This wasn't the comfort of her day to day. Suddenly she felt the pressure that everyone would be looking at her as the expert.

How about you? What would push you into that panic zone? Being asked to get up on stage in front of one hundred people? Most of us would go straight to the outer circle of our panic zone, even if the subject was something we were comfortable having a one-to-one conversation about.

I heard a great analogy once: *"Your comfort zone is like knicker elastic! Once you stretch it, it never goes back to the exact same size."*

The great thing about Beth's story is that she had a choice. She could have said a polite no thank you or she could have said yes.

She decided to say yes! I love that. We had a conversation and I helped her to prepare, both what she was going to say out loud and what she would say to herself beforehand (as both are important).

She said yes, she prepared and she did it. Did she love it? No. But she didn't die and she didn't get laughed at. And they asked her to come back a year later. Again, she said yes and this time she did enjoy it.

— **What could you say yes to?**

It is worth knowing that there is something that surrounds your comfort zone. Imagine it as a line all the way around it. That something is fear! All you need to do is make a tiny little hole that pierces it. On the other side, in those stretch and panic zones, is growth.

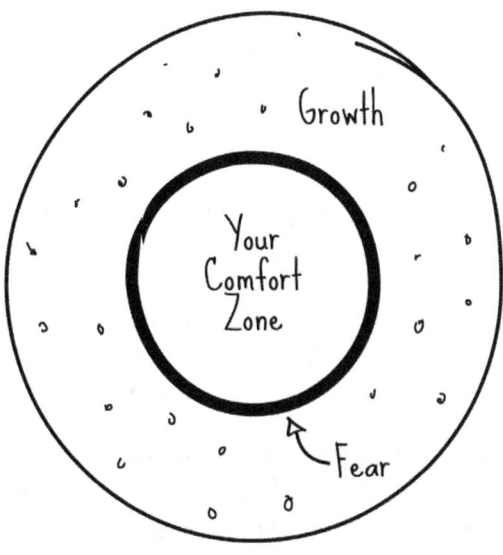

EXERCISE:

— How can you step out of your comfort zone in order to grow?

— When can you do it?

Each time you stretch your comfort zone it will get bigger and bigger, and on the other side is pure growth.

YOU CAN BE ANYTHING YOU WANT

I said earlier that I love setting goals but I never used to. How about you? Do you love or hate setting them?

This is what changed for me. If you currently occupy the 'I hate setting goals' camp, this may inspire you to think differently, to be more open to change and what's achievable for you if you too set goals that excite you.

For years I didn't know what I wanted from my career. I showed up, tried to do a good job, and I got rewarded for it through new opportunities and promotions.

In 2009, I was offered a promotion that felt huge. I remember saying to my husband shortly before getting married that I had reached my potential. That was it! There would be no more promotions, no more pay rises. In hindsight, I believed this partly because I didn't believe in myself (my inner critic was way too loud) and I didn't have anything I was aiming for.

Then a couple of things changed. First, I got a boss who helped me think about me. He helped me realise what I was good at, helped me to see my potential, and helped me figure out my values and what was important to me.

I am a firm believer that the more you know about you, what you're good at, what triggers you and what you want in life, the more successful you will be.

The other thing is that I met a mentor, someone who started asking me what job I wanted in the future. The future? I had no idea! Surely, I'd just carry on going to work and doing a good job?

They planted the seed that I would make a great Commercial Director. I had never heard of this role before and it didn't exist in the company I worked for, but I googled it and found that I loved the idea of the job description. It felt way above where I was right then, but suddenly I had something to aim for and it changed me.

I started thinking about what my future could look like; I felt excited for what I could achieve. I was no longer just turning up and doing a good job. I knew who I was, what motivated me and what I was aiming for.

A couple of things followed this. First, I became a Commercial Sales Director three years later. Second, I left my corporate job in 2023 to be the CEO of my own business. This was fourteen years after I told my husband I had reached my peak. I left corporate earning ten times what I had earned in 2009.

Think big. You don't need to know how it could happen but give yourself something to aim for by setting some exciting goals.

EXERCISE:

Spend time thinking about what excites you about your future. Perhaps you have a dream job, a dream house, a dream lifestyle or a dream business you want to start. Allow yourself to aim big.

— **What excites you about your future?**

SUMMARY - EXCITING GOALS

When you set and achieve goals, you feel a sense of accomplishment. You have more hope and you feel more confident and optimistic for the future.

Set yourself goals that excite you and that you *want* to achieve and see how far you can fly.

The exercises we went through that can help you are:

1. Remember life is too short for sevens. What do you feel you should do that you are ready to say no to?
2. How and when can you stretch out of your comfort zone? Your comfort zone will grow; beyond it is pure growth.
3. What excites you about your future?

To help you to set Exciting goals, write down:

— **What do you want to give ten out of ten to?**

S — STRENGTHEN WITH HOPE

A huge part of confidence is about hope: hope that you can achieve what you want; hope that you are doing the right things and doing a good job; hope that what you are doing is making a difference; hope that you can do what you want to do.

Lots of research has been done around hope. People who have hope have increased job satisfaction, increased happiness, more resilience, increased performance, and less anxiety.

Would you like this to describe you? Yes? Then strengthening your exciting goals with hope is crucial.

In Part Three of this book, we will look at hope in even more detail so you close this book knowing you can achieve all you want. First, here are a few more stories and questions you can ask yourself.

WHAT IS THE WORST THAT CAN HAPPEN?

Before we hear from one of our cast of characters, here is a story from my own experience.

Imagine being eighteen, landing your first full time job and living your dream of working in London. Even better, everyone tells you how great you're doing – your boss, your peers and those you work with all agree that you're fantastic at your job.

You earn £12,500 per year and it is time for your first ever pay rise. With all this positive feedback, surely it is time to 'show me the money'!

You are passed an envelope that says thank you for all hard work, we're pleased to give you a two percent pay rise. £250 a year doesn't quite shout, "We value you so much."

What would you do? Thank them and leave? Or say something?

I decided right there and then to say something. I wasn't rude, entitled or angry. However, I chose to ask myself, what was the worst that could happen and say something. The conversation went something like this:

Me: Thank you for this. However, I'm quite surprised.
Boss: Right, how come?
Me: Well, you've been telling me all year what a good job I've been doing. I don't feel that this pay rise of £250 matches the feedback I've been given and the amount of effort I put in.
Boss: Ok, what were you hoping for?
Me: Well, I was hoping for £1,500.
Boss: Leave it with me and I'll come back to you.

I'm sure the conversation was slightly different, but this is how I remember it twenty-four years later. I wasn't emotional, rude or self-righteous. I was honest.

Guess what happened. Two days later, they called me in and handed me a new envelope with a £1,500 pay rise written on the letter.

You will not get every single thing you ask for, but if you don't ask, you definitely won't get what you want. I knew if I was polite and honest, they wouldn't turn around and fire me on the spot. The worst that could have happened was that they'd say no.

What would you love to have the confidence to ask for or do? How can you ask for it without being rude? How can you go for it without endangering yourself?

Ask yourself: what is the worst that can happen?

If you feel worried, allow yourself to properly think about what the worst-case scenario could be. In this situation, the worst-case would be that they'd say no. When you think about it, often the worst-case isn't actually that bad.

I once heard, when you're worrying about something, ask if there is an immediate and positive action you can take. If yes, then go do it. If no, then there is no benefit from worrying, so try to let it pass.

Here is a story to help you think of some immediate positive actions you could take.

Maria wanted to push out of her comfort zone by doing more public speaking, so she said yes to talking at an event run by her company's women's network. She felt extremely nervous and I could tell she was worried that the worst case might come true. For her the worst case was that she would forget what she was meant to say.

I helped her by asking her two questions.

First: "If the worst-case happened, how would you handle it?"

After reflecting she said, "I'd probably stop, take a deep breath, have a sip of water, tell everyone I felt nervous and share a story I'm planning on telling them which I feel comfortable saying as I've told it a hundred times."

Then I asked, "How can you try and stop the worst case from happening?"

This question sparked her to say, "I could take some notes with me, practise before and listen to my inner cheerleader before getting up to speak."

It was amazing how much better she felt by thinking about the immediate, positive actions she could take instead of worrying about the worst case.

In my example of asking for a pay rise, the worst case was that they would say no. If it did happen, how would I have handled it? I would have said thank you for considering it and walked away. It would have been up to me if I then chose to move companies because of it.

How could I stop the worst case from happening? By doing research on the market rate for similar roles and asking for feedback from people I worked with to be able to quote them.

EXERCISE:

When you next do something that feels brave, to boost your confidence ask yourself:

— **What is the worst that could happen?**

— How would you handle it if the worst case really did happen?

— What can you do so the worst case hopefully doesn't happen?

IS IT TIME TO REINVENT YOURSELF?

Confidence is a funny thing. What gives you a little boost in confidence may be completely different from what works for someone else.

What (other than listening to your inner cheerleader) helps elevate your confidence?

I only ever wear my wedding rings when I leave the house (which doesn't happen that often because I work from home on video calls every day). However, I also put them on when I deliver a virtual workshop. It may sound strange, but part of my ritual to boost my confidence before delivering a workshop, whether there are ten or six hundred people, is to put on my rings, some lipstick and a spray of perfume. (No idea why I think perfume will help on a video call, but it does.) All these things give me a little boost that I know helps me to perform at my best.

What about you? What gives you that boost? Is it a certain outfit, shoes, jewellery, a watch, perfume or aftershave or having your hair in a certain style?

When I returned from maternity leave for the second time, I felt a big boost in confidence that was partly linked to how I looked and partly to a newfound determination. Before then my career had progressed nicely (my inner critic will tell you that is because I was lucky) and I enjoyed work, but I had no idea when my luck would run out.

But something changed during that year off with my youngest. I spent some of the time reflecting on who I was, what I enjoyed doing, what I was good at and wondering what could happen next in my career.

I made a decision. I was going to return to work dressing for the job I wanted.

For years, the 'work uniform' I had fallen into was simply black trousers, ballet pump flat shoes, a delicate necklace, a nondescript top and hair tied up when I couldn't be bothered to wash it.

In May 2014, I decided my new 'work uniform' would consist of dresses, heels, chunky jewellery and always wearing my hair down (freshly washed!). Fast forward a few years and post Covid, I have to say that I rarely bother with heels, and smart trainers are just as good, but I became conscious of how I wanted to come across.

I love helping people think about their personal brand. I often say, "You have a personal brand whether you want one or not, because a brand is simply what people say about you when you're not in the room." A lot of your brand is about how you act and show up, but it is also linked to how you look and the impression you give others.

EXERCISE:

To help build your hope and boost your confidence, think about these questions:

— **What do you want people to say about you when you're not in the room?**

— **How do you want to show up?**

— **What little tweaks can you make to help boost your confidence?**

TELL YOURSELF SOMETHING THAT IS TRUE AND POSITIVE

What do you say to yourself before doing something you are nervous about? Do you listen to your inner critic or your inner cheerleader?

Jada was preparing for a big presentation. She knew what she wanted to say, had written her slides and was prepared, but she felt sick with nerves. Ever felt like this?

We spoke a few days before she was due on stage and I asked her, "What story are you telling yourself?" Her answer was, "I might make a fool of myself. I might forget what I'm planning on saying. What if I do it badly?" This was definitely a case of her inner critic doing all the talking.

It is great to tune into what your inner critic is saying, because when you do, you bring those fears up from your subconscious into your conscious and then you can start to challenge them.

"What can you tell yourself that's true and positive?" I asked Jada.

If I had said, "What can you tell yourself that's more positive," she may have said, "This is going to be the best presentation anyone's ever seen and I'm definitely going to get a standing ovation." Yes, that is positive but is it true and is it likely?

It is important for us to tell ourselves something that is both *true* and positive, because our brains are clever. Jada's brain, like your brain knows when things are made up and not true, so simply thinking positively doesn't work or help, because you won't believe it.

Instead, think of things that are true *and* positive, such as, "I've prepared a good presentation, I know what I'm going to say, no one listening wants me to do a bad job and I am safe." Your brain can't argue, because it is true. You may still feel scared, but by telling yourself something true and positive, you will feel calmer and therefore you will do a better job than if you walk on stage worried you will make a fool of yourself.

Jada and I had an hour together during which she shared what she was planning on saying to those in the audience, but also what she was going to say inwardly to herself. Don't underestimate the importance of that inner talk.

I messaged her afterwards asking how it went and she replied that although she was nervous, people told her that they connected so much with what she said and she was an 'inspiration'. She felt great.

How can you build hope that you will be good at whatever it is you're nervous about?

— **What can you tell yourself that is true and positive?**

Jada's story may resonate with you, but in case it feels a bit distant because you never need to (or want to) stand on stage, here is another story.

Think again about Lucy's weekly spelling test at school.

Every Monday morning, she goes into school knowing she will be tested on the ten spellings she learnt and practised that weekend.

If you are her parent or carer, you have three choices of what you say to her as she heads into school.

1. You can be her critic.
2. You can talk positively.

3. You can say something that is true *and* positive.

Let's take them one by one for her situation.

1. You can be her critic and say: "Good luck with your spelling test today, but you probably won't do very well. The words are extremely hard, and remember that time that you only got two out of ten?"
2. You can talk positively and say: "Good luck with your spelling test today, you're going to get every single one right, be top of the class and the teacher will probably give you an award for being so amazing."
3. Or you can say something true *and* positive: "Good luck with your spelling test today, you did really well when we were practising them and you've memorised the trickier words."

Which would you choose? Probably number three, right? Things that are true and positive so she feels good walking into school.

You probably read number one and thought, who would say that to their child? But most people talk to themselves like that all the time. We talk to others, whether that's our kids, friends or colleagues in a far kinder way than we talk to ourselves.

You would never tell your best friend they will be rubbish at a test, at a presentation, at their new job. But I bet you've told *yourself* plenty of times you're rubbish, you'll do a bad job and you'll fail.

Laying it out like this hopefully allows you to see things clearer. It is easy to default to listening to your critic... or you can choose to say something to yourself that is both true and positive which will give you a boost of confidence, positivity and hope.

EXERCISE:

— **What are you feeling nervous about?**

— **What can you say to yourself that is both true *and* positive?**

SUMMARY - STRENGTHEN WITH HOPE

When you have more hope, you have increased job satisfaction, increased happiness, more resilience, increased performance and less anxiety.

The exercises we went through that can help you are:

1. To boost your confidence when you do something brave, ask yourself: What's the worst that could happen? How would you handle it if the worst case did happen? And what can you do so the worst case doesn't happen?
2. Think about how you want to show up. What little tweaks can you make to help boost your confidence?
3. What is one thing you can tell yourself that is both true and positive?

To help you to Strengthen with hope, write down:

— **What is true and positive for you?**

SUMMARY - YOUR CONFIDENCE RULES

You have completed Your Confidence Rules: the simple steps you can take, the questions you can ask yourself and the exercises you can do so you can boost your confidence.

They are simple, yes, but not always easy to do. Have you taken the time to answer each question as you go through this book or have you skimmed over certain questions?

Pause and take a moment longer to reflect. Take the time to find your answers to these questions and watch your confidence grow.

Which stories did you love about Confidence? What are your takeaways from this collection of stories? What do you want to remind yourself of? Which tools are you going to put into practice?

— **Write down what you want to remember:**

Don't forget you can download a worksheet on
Your Confidence Rules here:
https://www.tararulecoaching.com/book-downloads plus there is a video from me which may help you further.

Your Confidence Rules:

Remember what you are good at.
Use your strengths.
Large vision.
Exciting goals.
Strengthen with hope.

Remember what you are good at. Know what your strengths are, whether they are skills, qualities or characteristics. Knowing what you're good at and using those strengths will help you feel happier and be more successful. It is time to own your strengths!

— **What are three of your strengths?**

Use your strengths. The more you use your strengths, the better you'll be, the more productive you'll be, the more energy you'll have, the more enthusiasm you'll have, and the better and more confident you'll feel. Turn your strengths into superpowers by using them more often.

— **When can you use your strengths tomorrow?**

Large vision. When you visualise something, it influences your subconscious, making you feel more motivated, focused and confident. You are much more likely to achieve it when you envision it. Get excited about what is possible, what your best possible life looks like and go after it with a new, fun energy.

— **What excites you about your future?**

Exciting goals. When you set and achieve goals you feel a sense of accomplishment. You have more hope for the future and you feel more confident and optimistic. Set yourself some goals that excite you and you want to achieve and see how far you can fly.

— **What do you want to give ten out of ten to?**

Strengthen with hope. When you have more hope, you have increased job satisfaction, increased happiness, more resilience, increased performance, and less anxiety. Who wants some of that? Talk to yourself as if you were talking to your best friend and start believing.

— **What is true and positive for you?**

I have another question for you.

— **How would you score your confidence out of ten now?**

One means you have no confidence, you doubt yourself all the time, you feel like you're constantly apologising, you question yourself and are not sure what you're doing or why. Ten means you feel great and you ooze confidence.

Now take a look back to the start of Your Confidence Stories. How has your score changed?

I would love to know how your score has changed during this section of the book and which of the Rules resonated most with you. Feel free to get in contact and let me know. (You can see where to find me at the end of this book.)

PART THREE

WHAT'S NEXT?

Imagine a future, your future. A future where you are happy, confident and full of energy. You no longer feel you need to apologise; you are kind to yourself, you sound confident and you feel confident too. You put into practice all that you've learnt and you listen to your inner cheerleader every day.

How does it feel?

Really imagine your future. What do you look like? How are you standing? Who are you with? What are you wearing? What are you doing? What habits have you created? Take a few deep breaths, close your eyes, and really feel it.

Remember this feeling, because it is all possible. You get to choose to be confident, you get to choose to stop apologising, you get to choose to listen to your inner cheerleader. And I'm so excited for you.

At the very start of the book, I gave you permission to stop apologising. I said it was ok to stop saying sorry, ok to feel more confident, ok to be you! How do you feel now? Do you feel like you have permission?

— What do you want to remind yourself of right now?

You could also benefit from revisiting some of the ideas in this book after you have made a few months' progress. New ideas will jump out at you and you will be reminded of important things.

In Part Three, I invite you to make one commitment to yourself.

WHAT'S YOUR COMMITMENT TO YOURSELF?

Throughout this book, I have referred to different Rules to help you to create Your Rule Book™. The final step of each of the Rules is critical, and they all have a theme.

The S in Your Confidence Rules is to Strengthen With Hope.
The S in Your Mindset Rules is to Strengthen With Commitment.
And the S in Your Apologising Rules is to Start Now.

Deciding what you want to do differently, how you're going to do it and starting it is crucial. I can't stress it enough.

You can hear inspirational stories, learn great tools, understand why you apologise and know how you could be more confident. But if you don't do anything with it, then nothing will change.

"NOTHING CHANGES IF NOTHING CHANGES"

- Courtney C. Stevens

Take a moment to reflect.

What is your commitment to yourself having almost finished this book? What can you do differently? What do you choose to do differently? What do you want to remind yourself of in six months' time?

This commitment is not to me, it is to you. Make it count because *you* matter and don't ever forget that.

WHAT'S YOUR COMMITMENT TO YOURSELF?

What is your commitment to yourself?

Your commitment could be to listen to your inner cheerleader more, to put some of the apologising tools into practice, to introduce these concepts to your kids to help the next generation or to remember what you are good at and use your strengths.

It could be something big or something that feels like the first step. It could be that you want to commit to lots of things or one. Take a moment to write it down.

— What is your commitment to yourself?

How does it feel to pause and decide what your commitment is, even if you can't see to the other side yet?

I would love to hear your commitments, so get in contact with me and let me know so I can celebrate with you.

LET'S BUILD SOME MORE HOPE TOGETHER

Congratulations for making your commitment to yourself. Let's take it one step further now and build some hope that you *will* achieve your commitment. When you have hope, when you believe you *can* achieve something, you are far more likely to achieve it. This part of the book is intended to help you go from feeling inspired to taking inspired action.

"HOPE IS NOT A STRATEGY."

- U.S. Army General Gordon Sullivan

I used to hear General Gordon's words in my corporate job all the time. You can't hope to hit the number that quarter, you can't hope that a launch will go well, you can't hope that you'll get a promotion one day. While this is all true, hope is important. I shared with you earlier the research around hope, but it's so important I'll share it again.

LET'S BUILD SOME MORE HOPE TOGETHER

Research shows that when you have hope you have increased job satisfaction, increased happiness, more resilience, increased performance, and less anxiety.

When you have hope, you look to the future with more optimism, you focus on possibilities rather than failures, and you are more excited for what is to come, so you are more likely to overcome obstacles and achieve your goals. This in turn gives you a sense of accomplishment. The more you feel this sense of accomplishment, the more hope you have that you will achieve the next goal you set yourself. This causes an upward spiral of positivity.

One of my favourite coaching sessions that I run in my group program is when we do a Hope Map together. Now we will build your hope, so you *will* stop apologising, so you *will* silence your inner critic, so you *will* find your confidence, so you *will* stop saying sorry.

You read in Part One that my inner critic would say to me, "You're not an entrepreneur," all the time and I managed to switch this to, "I have loads of entrepreneurial qualities." I switched my mindset, but what else?

I started visualising my future, what my perfect day could look like, I built a plan, I figured out my why and had hope that I could make it work.

I now *know* I am a successful entrepreneur. I have my own business, I coach amazing people, I am flown around the world to deliver workshops, I make a difference. I made my dream and vision a reality.

The most important things I had were belief and hope. I figured out what I needed to do, what could stop me, what obstacles could get in my way and how I could overcome them. I built hope!

You can download Your Hope Map here:
https://www.tararulecoaching.com/book-downloads.
Fill it in as we work through it now.

There are eight steps, so let's start with step one.

STEP 1 - SET AN EXCITING GOAL

Choose one goal you would like to set yourself after reading this book. What one thing do you want to do more of or differently? What is your one commitment to yourself?

Perhaps it is to stop saying sorry so much, to stop saying a specific phrase like, "Sorry this might be a stupid question." It could be to listen to your inner cheerleader every day, to stop being so hard on yourself, to feel more confident.

At one of my virtual retreats, my clients spent two hours thinking about and getting excited about their goals for the year. Do not skip over this goal setting step too quickly. Think of something that excites you.

You could think about your goal to stop apologising or to increase your confidence.

You could think about the different areas of your life, like financial, personal, career/business, health. See what goals excite you in each of these quadrants.

An exercise we did at the retreat which people loved was to write down these words:

Wouldn't it be fun if...

We wrote as many sentences as possible starting with the words, "Wouldn't it be fun if..." Here are some that clients have shared with me in the past to give you some inspiration.

Wouldn't it be fun if I travelled through Europe.
Wouldn't it be fun if I had a role where I inspired others.
Wouldn't it be fun if I owned a coffee shop.
Wouldn't it be fun if I was a Director.
Wouldn't it be fun if I bought a plot of land.
Wouldn't it be fun if I earned enough money that I could buy

my parents' house for them.

I did this exercise for the first time four years ago. I wrote a whole page and here are a few of mine. Some of them have come true already and some haven't (yet) but I know, and have hope, that they will:

Wouldn't it be fun if I wrote a book.
Wouldn't it be fun if my job was coaching.
Wouldn't it be fun if I earned more money, running my own business, than I do in my corporate job.
Wouldn't it be fun if I did a TED talk.

Here is some space to write your 'wouldn't it be fun ifs'

— **Wouldn't it be fun if...**

Looking at these and reflecting on what you've taken from this book so far, what is your one goal that you'd love to build some hope towards right now?

— **My one goal is...**

STEP 2 - WHAT ARE YOU AIMING TOWARDS?

Once you have your goal, make sure that goal is something you can aim *towards* instead of something you want to move *away from*.

If your goal is 'don't apologise', it is something you want to move away from. However, your brain doesn't actually hear the negative words like *don't* and *not*. So, for 'don't apologise' your brain only hears 'apologise' which lead to you apologising more! Instead, make it something you can aim towards, using positive language like 'sound more assertive'.

The same is true for kids. Their brains often ignore the word *don't*. Instead of saying, "Don't run," try saying, "Walk," and instead of, "Don't touch the hot plate," say, "Keep your hands clear as the plate is hot."

It is also important to set yourself exciting goals. Goals you want to achieve, that make you feel good, that motivate you and ignite your passion. This energy comes more from aiming *towards* goals rather than away from them.

Let's take a look at the goal you set yourself in step one.

Do you need to reframe it so you are aiming towards it?

Here are some examples for you:

LET'S BUILD SOME MORE HOPE TOGETHER

Goals you're moving away from	Goals you're aiming towards
Stop apologising.	Sound more assertive.
Don't let my inner critic take over.	Listen to my inner cheerleader more.
Don't let fear hold me back.	Believe in myself.
Stop being so hard on myself.	Be kind to myself.
Don't work such long hours.	Have a good work life balance.
Don't let old feedback hold me back.	Choose what I believe and how I show up.

— What goal are you aiming towards?

STEP 3 - WHY?

Knowing your why is critical but people often miss it out.

Research shows that if you don't know your why, it is harder to maintain motivation when things get tough. And it will get tough! So often, I see people defining their goal, identifying the steps they want to take and start taking action without thinking about their why. When it gets tough, they give up.

Let's think about the goal many people set themselves, often multiple times a year. You may have set yourself this goal before. That goal is to lose weight. You set your goal to lose weight. You know that if you eat less and move more, you will do it.

You start. But after a few weeks or a few days, or maybe even a few hours (tell me I'm not the only person who only lasts a few hours), you give up. You lost motivation. However, if you think about your why, you are much more likely to achieve it.

Your why could be to feel fit and healthy, to set a good example for your kids, to feel confident in your clothes, to live to see your grandchildren, to run around in the garden with your kids, to feel more energised or to sleep better. You are different from everyone else in the world so your why will be different.

You may think your goal is to lose weight, but it's often so much more than that, deeper than that. It is often about health, feeling fitter, living better, living longer. The deeper, more emotional and personal you get, the better, as you are more likely to do something when you remember why you're doing it.

Find and connect with your emotional anchor.

If your goal is to sound more assertive... Why?

It probably goes so much deeper than sounding assertive. What is the bigger picture for you? Why do you want to sound more assertive? What will this give you? Your why could be so you demonstrate assertiveness to your kids, so you are taken more seriously at work, so you make more of an impact.

If your goal is to believe in yourself... Why?

Your why could be so you feel happier at work, so you reach your potential, so you go for that promotion which will enable you to live your dream life.

What is your why for the goal you set yourself in Step two?

— **What is your why?**

STEP 4 - WHAT ARE YOUR PATHWAYS?

The next step is to plan how you can achieve that goal. What are the different pathways you could take? Pathways are simply the different ways you could achieve your goal. You do not need to commit right now. Allow yourself to think big over the next few steps and get creative. Here are some questions to help you think big.

— What have you tried in the past that worked?

— What have you tried in the past that hasn't worked?

— Who do you know that has achieved a similar goal? What do you think they did?

— Feel free to ask other people for ideas too. What do they suggest?

— What tools have you learnt in this book that you could put into practice?

If your goal is to sound more assertive, then how? Start getting specific. You could:

- Re-read emails before you send them to remove any 'little words'.
- Write a list of when you say sorry out of habit and decide what you'd like to replace it with.
- Tune into your inner cheerleader by starting every day telling yourself something true and positive, which will help you stay motivated and uplifted.

If your goal is to believe in yourself, then how?

- Wake up every morning and say something kind to yourself.
- Every time you become aware of your inner critic taking over, thank it and remember it is trying to keep you safe.
- Remember what you are good at and use your strengths when you find something hard.

— **What are your pathways? Think of at least three ways you could achieve your goal.**

STEP 5 - WHAT ARE THE OBSTACLES?

Great, you've got a few ideas of what you could do. Let's think of the obstacles now. What could stop you from doing or achieving each of those pathways?

It may sound counter intuitive. We are talking about building hope that you will achieve your goal but now we are thinking about what could go wrong! If you just have an idea of what you can do to achieve your goal and you go for it, when things get difficult (which they will at some point) you are more likely to stop and say, "Well that didn't work."

By considering what could go wrong you can plan for how to overcome these obstacles.

If your pathway was to re-read emails to check for 'little words' before sending, what could go wrong?

- You have to send something urgently so you don't have time.
- You're not totally sure what words to check for.
- You forget!

If your pathway was to wake every morning and say something kind to yourself, your obstacles could be:

- You have a bad night sleep and wake up feeling grumpy.
- Your alarm doesn't go off, so you are running late before you even start.
- You forget again.

For each of the pathways you wrote down in step four:

— **What obstacles could you face? What could stop you?**

STEP 6 - WHAT ARE YOUR PATHWAYS? (AGAIN)

Perfect. You have thought of all that could go wrong and what could get in your way. Now, how could you overcome each of those obstacles? Think about these pathways now, when your rational brain is in control, rather than waiting to be in the moment when your emotional brain takes over.

Building on the example in step five about re-reading emails to check for 'little words' before sending…

The first obstacle was that you have to send something urgently so you don't have time.

A way you could overcome this is to ensure you at least read the opening line. Does the word 'sorry' appear in the first line? If yes, delete it before sending.

If you are not totally sure what words to check for, you could go into your sent items and look at the last few emails you sent, especially those you sent to people who may trigger you. Read through and spot what words you see repeatedly. Write them all down in a list. What could you replace them with? Or could you delete them altogether? You have now created your checklist.

The other example was related to wanting to start the day by saying something kind to yourself, but you have a bad night's sleep or you wake up late. If this happens, it is even more important. Remember the importance of boosting your positive emotions and needing three positive emotions for every negative. You can also do something called habit stacking which James Clear talks about in his book *Atomic Habits*. You stack a new habit on top of an existing habit. Every morning you open the curtains, have a shower and brush your teeth, so attach the new habit to one of those and you are far more likely to stick to it.

LET'S BUILD SOME MORE HOPE TOGETHER

Finally, an obstacle for both was that you forget! This one is real for us all. We have the best intentions, we feel fired up and ready to go but then we forget. Here are a few things you can do to create a new habit.

1. Remember your why. The more personal you can make it the better.
2. Give your brain a prompt. Many years ago, I got feedback that I looked way too serious when I presented, so I wrote the word 'smile' on a post-it note and stuck it next to the camera. I trained myself and now I smile on camera without thinking. If you want to start reading at bedtime, you are more likely to do it if you prompt your brain by putting the book on your pillow in the morning so you see it at bedtime, rather than relying on your brain to remember later.
3. Reward yourself when you do it. Play a song that makes you feel good, step away from your desk for a few minutes, tell a friend and celebrate what you've done. It doesn't matter how you celebrate, but allow yourself to recognise you have done something good. It will give you a huge boost but we rarely do it.

While it is great to think about the big pathways, the big steps, they are just that. Big! When things get tough, when you feel you don't have time and are juggling things, it is often the big things that we drop. The micro steps are equally important.

If you have a goal to put yourself out there and talk more in meetings…

A big step may be volunteering to lead a session in your team meeting or saying yes when asked to do a presentation.

Micro steps could include switching your video on during the next video call, coming off mute and joining in with the small talk at the start of a meeting or asking a question.

These are all micro steps that add up and help you feel more confident that you can achieve the big steps.

— **How can you overcome your obstacles?**

— **What are the micro steps you can take?**

STEP 7 - WHAT SUPPORT DO YOU NEED?

What help and support do you need to help you achieve your goal? It could be a person, a tool or a system you need to put in place.

Perhaps you need to have a conversation with a family member, a colleague or your boss about what you are aiming towards and ask for their help and support. Maybe a coach will help you overcome your mindset obstacles.

Do you need a tool of some sort – an app or a program that will make your life easier and better enable you to achieve what you are aiming towards?

Is there a system or process you can implement to help you? Even something as simple as putting thirty minutes in your diary once per month to reflect on how you are doing against your goals can help.

I do this last one every month. I have thirty minutes in my diary, time blocked for reflections on the first working day of each month. It sets me up brilliantly for the month and helps me remember what is important to me rather than getting lost and prioritising things that don't matter.

You can download a PDF of Your Reflections and Goals here: https://www.tararulecoaching.com/book-downloads

Remember Neesha, who wanted to stop apologising when dinner was ready, to stop saying, "Sorry dinner is late"? I asked her what she thought would help her to kick the habit. She told me, "Accountability. I don't have a personal to-do list so I don't prioritise changing habits. I need a personal to-do list and someone checking in."

She needed a tool to capture her personal to-do list. A piece of paper or an online tool is a personal preference. Neesha needed to put a system in place, i.e. every Monday having ten minutes in her diary to write her personal to-do list and every Friday ten minutes to review it and celebrate the small wins. And finally, a person holding her accountable, a friend or coach checking in with her to see how she was doing against her goal.

— **What support do you need to help you achieve what you are aiming towards? To help you achieve your exciting goal?**

KEEP HOLD OF THE MONKEY

When you think about support, especially when you're looking at getting support from other people, think about who is holding the monkey (the responsibility). You, your boss, your partner, your coach?

I first heard this expression eight years ago when I took my first step towards learning about coaching but it is also relevant if you're a leader or when you're thinking about your own personal development.

As a coach, my job is to help you to reflect, to give you time to think, to hold the mirror up, to help you come up with the answers, and to help you *feel* accountable. My job as a coach is not to give you the answers, to make you do something or to *make* you accountable.

Imagine you asked me to coach you to help you with your confidence.

The thing you want help with is your confidence, that's the monkey! You sit down and say, "I want you to help me be

LET'S BUILD SOME MORE HOPE TOGETHER

more confident," and you pass the monkey to me. You pass the issue, the problem or the question to me.

I have a choice. I can either accept that monkey and feel responsible for making sure you feel more confident by the end of our session together. Or I can pass that monkey straight back to you.

You may think I should keep that monkey and help you. But in fact, the moment you relinquish responsibility and feel like it is my issue to fix, you are actually less likely to achieve your goal because you no longer feel responsible. You let yourself off the hook by passing it over to me.

I want you to solve it and feel more confident, so I need to pass that monkey straight back to you. I do this by asking you questions rather than giving you answers, by holding the mirror up to what you say and help you think about how you can achieve your goals in new ways.

You walk out of our coaching session feeling like you are holding the monkey and are responsible for the next steps. You know it is on you to put into practice what we talked about. This is so much more powerful than walking out thinking I am holding the monkey and am going to 'fix' everything for you.

Keep hold of your monkey! It is great to have support, to have a coach, to ask for feedback, to figure out the accountability that's right for you. But please, please, please. Keep hold of that monkey and see how many more actions you take.

STEP 8 - YOUR COMMITMENTS

And now to the final step.

What are you actually going to do? When you started thinking about pathways, I invited you to think big. Hopefully you've taken that through the whole of this exercise. And now it is commitment time. What *will* you do? What are you committed to doing?

You may have written lots of pathways both big and micro, which is fantastic, but please don't feel overwhelmed or that you need to implement them all straight away. Often, we find it hard to change more than a couple of things at a time so take it easy.

Be kind to yourself. Decide up to three things you want to commit to.

Once you have done them, come back and take a look at what else you wrote down so you can choose your next few steps that you're committed to.

Take a moment now and write down your commitments.

— **What will you do?**

Finally, *when* will you put them into action? It is one thing to say what you will do, but by taking immediate action towards them you are far more likely to keep that momentum up.

"SOMEDAY IS NOT A DAY OF THE WEEK."

- *Janet Dailey*

When will you take action? Instead of thinking one day, someday, next month or next week, taking action in the next twenty-four hours will help you massively.

— **When will you take action?**

All these steps are covered in Your Hope Map, which is a one-page worksheet that helps you work through all these steps and means you can create one for each goal you set yourself. It makes it easier to refer back to them too.

I even completed one myself six months ago about my goal to write this book. The process helped me identify that fear could get in my way if I let it, that the first thing I wanted to do was write the outline of this book and I wanted to remember my strengths each time I wrote.

You can download Your Hope Map here: https://www.tararulecoaching.com/book-downloads

THE END IS JUST THE BEGINNING

Congratulations. Through this book you have been on a journey to create Your Rule Book™. You created Your Mindset Rules in Part One. You created Your Confidence Rules in Part Two. And through the whole book we've been building Your Apologising Rules.

Let's take a look now at a summary of Your Apologising Rules, the simple steps you can take and the questions you can ask yourself so that you stop apologising, silence your inner critic, find your confidence and stop saying sorry.

They are simple, yes, but as with the other Rules, they are not always easy to do. Have you spent time answering each question as you go through this book or have you skimmed any areas?

Pause and take a moment longer to reflect. Find your answers to these questions and watch your assertiveness grow. Although you are almost at the end of this book, it is not the end for you, it is just the beginning. By putting into practice everything that resonated with you, by listening to your inner cheerleader more, you can and will stop apologising and find your confidence.

Here is a summary of Your Apologising Rules which you've seen throughout the book. Don't forget you can download them here:
https://www.tararulecoaching.com/book-downloads

Your Apologising Rules:

Realise why.
Unpick it.
Listen to your inner cheerleader.
Establish your toolbox.
Start *now*.

Realise why. Right at the beginning of Part One we reflected on why you apologise, who you apologise to and what for. Is it a habit? Is it part of your identity? Is it due to feedback from years ago? Realising why you do it is the first crucial step.

— **Why do you apologise?**

Unpick it. We then went a level deeper and started to understand the beliefs you have formed. We met your inner critic and got creative on what they look, sound and feel like. What did you notice they are telling you? Maybe it is that you don't deserve a seat at the table, that other people are more important than you or you feel you need everyone to like you.

— **What are you telling yourself?**

Listen to your inner cheerleader. You then met your inner cheerleader and were invited to listen to them instead. You realised that your inner critic is trying to keep you comfortable and safe, but you can choose to say, "Thank you." You were invited to list out all the beliefs your inner critic was telling you and to reframe them by listening to your inner cheerleader.

— **What is your truth?**

Establish your toolbox. We then moved to Part Two where you heard lots of apologising stories which all had a tool, a framework or questions to help you reframe your language. Instead of only thinking 'well it's ok for them', make sure you choose the tools that resonate most for you so you can put them into practice.

— **What tools resonate for you that you can apply?**

Start now. Finally in Part Three, we focussed on what is next, making a commitment to yourself, building hope that you can achieve your exciting goals and deciding what and when you can start. My hope is that you have already started putting what you've learnt into practice and are applying it to your life.

— **When can you start using these tools and practice?**

I hope you finish this book full of inspiration but also ready to take inspired action.

Before we part ways, here are a couple of reminders to help you put all you have learnt into action and apply it to your own life.

CONSCIOUS COMPETENCE

About half way through this book you read about a concept called conscious competence. It is such a powerful concept that I am sharing a summary of it again with you now.

When you finish this book soon, you have two choices. You can finish and beat yourself up that you are not already applying all the tools immediately. Or you can finish and celebrate that you have taken a huge step towards switching how you talk both to yourself and to others.

Perhaps you are already using some of the tools; perhaps you are listening to your inner cheerleader more; perhaps you feel more confident already.

If so, well done. That's great. But! There will be moments when your inner critic takes over again, moments when you apologise and wonder why on earth you're doing it, and moments when you feel that inner confidence has completely disappeared again.

Why? Because you are human! It takes time and practice to create strong and healthy habits. Even though you now have so much awareness, you won't be perfect every time. (Sorry to any perfectionists reading this.)

So, here is a refresher on conscious competence.

When you learn something new, like learning to stop apologising, embracing a new belief or learning to drive, you go through four phases.

1. Unconscious incompetence.
2. Conscious incompetence.
3. Conscious competence.
4. Unconscious competence.

Let's remember how this concept works with learning to drive.

Before you learn, you are unconsciously incompetent; you don't realise that you don't know how to drive. When you get behind the wheel for the first time, reality hits you. You are consciously incompetent. After a few lessons, you move to being consciously competent, having to think about everything you do. Finally, once you have been driving for a while you reach the unconscious competence space and you drive without having to think about it.

In the early stages you make a choice to either give up or keep practising, knowing it will get easier.

Hearing this again, what do you want to remind yourself about the learning journey you are on? Remember to be kind to yourself, knowing you are on the right path to unconscious competence.

PRACTICE, PRACTICE, PRACTICE

One thing I would love you to take away from this book is the importance of practice. If you read a book about how to swim, yes, you could learn the theory and different techniques, but what will make the difference is the decision to get in that pool and start practising.

For you, you're reading this book to change how you talk, to stop apologising and feel more confident. While yes, reading through all the exercises to shift your mindset will help you massively, the breakthrough will come from putting them into practice.

When you look at your goals and reflections, what can you start practising straight away? What are your baby steps, the micro steps? How can you practise in a safe way?

Procrastination often gets in the way. Does it get in your way of success?

"PROCRASTINATION IS THE ENEMY OF SUCCESS

- Barbara Corcoran

People often procrastinate because they are scared of what might happen, so they stay in a state of indecision thinking 'one day' instead of 'today'.

We know that when you make a decision you feel happier, as you reduce your anxiety levels and therefore feel less stressed. So make the decision now to start.

Anastasia used to hate making decisions but I helped her feel happier and more comfortable with decision making. Instead of starting big and getting her to make decisions at work worth thousands of pounds, we started small. She practised in a safe space.

When we dug deeper on decisions she hated making, one of them was what she would have for dinner. When her partner said, "What do you fancy for dinner tonight?" she normally said, "I don't mind." We decided to start there. From then on, she made a decision and said what she wanted that day. It was key for her to get used to making decisions when it felt completely safe and there were no repercussions. She was stretching that decision-making muscle in her brain, knowing that when she got more comfortable making the smaller decisions, the bigger ones would feel easier too.

If one of your goals is to have the confidence to get on stage and present in front of two hundred people, know that you don't need to take the leap straight away. You can practise and build your way up.

How can you practice in a safe way?

Maybe your first step is to ask a question in a meeting, to present in a virtual meeting, to present in front of a small group, allowing yourself to grow in confidence before you get up in front of two hundred.

What goals have come through for you reading this book?

— **How can you practise in a safe way?**

Also think about asking someone to 'spot you', someone who you trust and value the opinion of. Tell them you are practising to sound more assertive or to sound more confident when you are presenting.

Who do you trust and value the opinion of? Who will be honest with you? Ask them for their feedback so you can grow even further.

RADICALLY COMMITTED

Let's finish this book being radically committed to stopping apologising and feeling more confident. By reading this book plus going through the Hope Map exercise in Part Three you are much closer to achieving your exciting goals.

Remember why you want this and feel energised for your future. Know the positive impact it will have on you, your life and those around you. Know you can achieve anything you want, especially when you listen to your inner cheerleader along the way.

When I decided I wanted to run my own business, I knew my biggest obstacle would be my belief in myself. So I prioritised strengthening it and listening to my inner cheerleader more.

I found out just how radically committed I was to my goal when my boss told me she was moving to America and asked if I was her backfill. This would have been a great opportunity, but I felt so calm when I said, "No thank you." I knew my future was coaching and I didn't want to change the path I was on. It felt great.

But a week later I panicked. My inner critic started doubting that I would be successful running my own business and instead wanted to stay nice and safe in my comfort zone.

I said, "Thank you," to Dobby and consciously decided to listen to my inner cheerleader who reminded me that I am a great coach, my business will be successful and I am good enough.

I put into practice all I have shared with you through this book. I remember how excited I was about my goal and deciding to be radically committed to making it happen.

Are you radically committed to achieving your exciting goals?

— Are you radically committed to stop apologising?

— Are you radically committed to find your confidence?

— And what does your inner cheerleader want to remind you?

THE END!

That leaves me to say well done for going on this journey. Well done for investing the time in you to silence your inner critic, find your confidence and stop saying sorry.

I set myself a goal six months ago to write a book that I love and I am pleased to say I have absolutely achieved that goal. I hope you have just finished reading a book that you love too.

I am excited for you to go forward with a newfound energy, focus and determination, knowing that if you dream something, you can make it happen. You have it within you to feel more confident and to stop saying sorry. Good luck!

HOW TO FIND ME

If you have loved this book (you've read all the way to the end so I'm assuming you have), here is how we can continue our journey together.

At the time of writing this book, I offer coaching, workshops and retreats. I coach one-to-one, in groups and have online programs. I run workshops for small team meetings all the way up to companywide masterclasses, both virtually, face to face and on stage. I run retreats in the UK, abroad and virtually.

What makes this even more exciting is that I know this will evolve and grow over time too, as I set myself new goals and continue stretching out of my comfort zone.

I would love you to reach out and let me know what resonated most with you, what your commitments are and what tools you are excited to put into practice.

Reach out too if you'd love to know how I can support you further, how we can work together or if you'd love me to run a workshop at your company.

Connect on LinkedIn:
https://www.linkedin.com/in/tararule/

Follow me on Instagram: @tararulecoaching
https://www.instagram.com/tararulecoaching/

Join my free Facebook group:
https://www.facebook.com/groups/busy2balanced/

Check out my website:
https://www.tararulecoaching.com

I send emails which aim to be a burst of positivity into your inbox every week so send me an email if you'd love to be added and receive yours too.

Email me: tara@tararule.co.uk

You can also download your free Prioritisation Toolbox: The ultimate prioritisation toolbox to give you more success, time and balance:
https://www.tararulecoaching.com/toolbox

And finally, a reminder where you can find all the resources that complement this book:
https://www.tararulecoaching.com/book-downloads

I look forward to hearing from you and continuing this journey with you.

Tara

x

ACKNOWLEDGEMENTS

I feel like I'm writing my Oscars speech and I worry I'm going to miss someone. Here goes.

Firstly, to my amazing girls, Sophia and Emilia. Sophia, thank you for all of our conversations about apologising which have inspired me to help even more people. And Emilia, thank you for helping me design my book cover. I love it and I love that you helped me design it. Girls, you are both amazing. I love you and am so incredibly proud of you both. To my amazing husband Steve who supported me leaving my nice safe corporate job last year to follow my dream. For still making my laugh after twenty years and for being the best husband I could ever wish for. I love you all to the moon and back!

To my mum and dad, thank you. I know you are both incredibly proud of me. Mum, thank you for listening to every single podcast interview I'm on, for reading every single article about me and for telling me how proud you are of me and how much you love me. And to my dad, before you passed away, you told me you knew I was destined for amazing things. You never knew I had this book idea in my head, but I know you'd agree that this is part of my journey of amazingness and impacting even more people. Thank you for believing in me, loving me and passing on to me your positivity. I love you and I miss you.

To my best friends where we live by #nojudging Carolyn and Jacqui, my positive ladies Nicola and Lindsay, Beth for being my biggest cheerleader, my amazing friend and COO Rachel. To Sarah who first pointed out to me that I have loads of entrepreneurial qualities. Who knew?! To my old boss, Claire, who helped me grow so much but also whose support was always unwavering. To Pete who believed in me when I had no idea what he saw in me. And to my amazing coaches Donna, Cheryl and Casey. I honestly wouldn't be where I am now without every single one of you.

Thank you to everyone I interviewed for this book, to those who told me they loved the idea years before I put pen to paper, my amazing clients who make my job the best job in the world and all who have supported my journey on social media. To Nick and Jacqui for helping me edit this book. To Nicky for creating such amazing images used throughout this book. And to all my friends who have been so supportive over coffee, dinner or cocktails throughout this book writing and entrepreneurial journey. Thank you for understanding that I couldn't name you all. (I actually wrote sorry for not naming you all, but realised I can't finish this book on an apology!)

And finally, to my editor Deanne. Seriously. You have been outstanding. I have loved being on this journey with you and I thank you, from the bottom of my heart. This book is a thousand times better thanks to our conversations, your help and your belief.

REFERENCES

Young, V (2011). *The Secret Thoughts of Successful Women.* Crown Business

Minter, H (2021). *WFH (Working From Home), How To Build A Career You Love When You're Not In The Office.* Greenfinch

Hendricks, G (2009). *The Big Leap.* HarperCollins Publishers

Peters, S (2012). *The Chimp Paradox: The Mind Management Programme to Help You Achieve Success, Confidence and Happiness.* Vermilion

Clear, J (2018) *Atomic Habits: An Easy & Proven Way to Build Good Habits & Break Bad Ones.* Penguin

ABOUT THE AUTHOR

Tara Rule is The Busy2Balanced Positive Psychology Coach who rose through the ranks at Adobe & O2 by writing her own Rule book.

She is now an international coach both in person and online, helping busy professionals, business owners and leaders to play to their strengths, succeed without sacrifice and create a life they love, so that they don't let fear get in the way of reaching their potential.

Tara understands how your inner voice can hold you back when it is just trying to keep you safe! She overcame hers, resulting in national press coverage which inspires others to grow their inner confidence and make amazing things happen.

She was a top-performing Commercial Director at the same time as having a young family and setting up her own business… she knows how to simplify the complex and what it takes to succeed.

She is a qualified Professional Coach and Positive Psychology Coach. When she works with you, she takes all this, plus her twenty years' experience working in corporate, to help you unlock your potential, find your balance and ignite your confidence, helping you create Your Rule Book™.

Tara lives what she preaches, achieving ambitious business goals while still feeling balanced – by leveraging her strengths, focused prioritisation, and taking inspired action.

She is often told she's a burst of positivity and she can't wait to inject your life with positivity, see your confidence grow and help you live your most fulfilling life.

www.ingramcontent.com/pod-product-compliance
Lightning Source LLC
Chambersburg PA
CBHW060103230426
43661CB00033B/1405/J